GOSPEL
THE BOOK OF
JOHN

Volumes in
Thomas Moore's
GOSPEL
New Translations with Commentary—
Jesus Spirituality for Everyone

THE BOOK OF MATTHEW

THE BOOK OF MARK

THE BOOK OF LUKE

THE BOOK OF JOHN

A NEW TRANSLATION WITH COMMENTARY—
JESUS SPIRITUALITY FOR EVERYONE

GOSPEL
THE BOOK OF
JOHN

THOMAS
MOORE

Walking Together, Finding the Way®
SKYLIGHT PATHS®
PUBLISHING
Nashville, Tennessee

SkyLight Paths Publishing
an imprint of Turner Publishing Company
Nashville, Tennessee
www.skylightpaths.com
www.turnerpublishing.com

Gospel—The Book of John:
A New Translation with Commentary—Jesus Spirituality for Everyone

Library of Congress Cataloging-in-Publication Data available upon request

ISBN 9781684425259   Paperback
ISBN 9781594736445   Hardback

Manufactured in the United States of America
Cover Design: Jenny Buono
Interior Design: Tim Holtz

To Bill and Lucy

Contents

Introduction to Gospel

Why a New Translation?

In my travels I have met many people who grew up hearing the Gospels in church and have now moved on in a different direction. Some have found their religion outmoded or just do not feel like participating any longer. Some have been offended, like many women who find formal religion sexist. Others are attracted to altogether different traditions, and some do not see the point of religion at all.

Many told me they missed the stories and the teachings, and wished they could have a better, more up-to-date understanding of them. I have heard from other people who did not have a Christian background and wondered if the Gospels could add to their more open-ended spiritual path. I have strong empathy for both positions and wanted to present the Gospels in a way that would speak to both.

Some Christians, both traditional and independent, expressed their fervent curiosity about how I might understand the teachings, given my unusual background as a monk, a student of world religions, and a depth psychotherapist. I felt their eagerness and sincerity when they asked me to recommend a good translation. I could not direct them without reservation to any translation that I knew and trusted, so the idea of my own version took root.

Another reason I felt it was time for a new version was my frustration at seeing faulty religious ideas, specifically about the teachings of Jesus, dragging down important political advances in our society. You do not have to look far beneath the headlines to see uninformed, emotional, and sentimental notions of Jesus's philosophy. Today we cannot afford to keep referring to outmoded and faulty versions of Jesus's teachings and using them to support questionable causes.

In the end, I wanted to make the Gospels accessible and attractive to all sorts of readers. I see no indication that Jesus intended to create a religion or a church. His purpose is clear: He wanted to raise human awareness and behavior to another level, where it would surpass its tendencies toward self-interest, xenophobia, greed, religious moralism, and an emphasis on insignificant rules. He imagined a more just and pleasurable world, a "kingdom of the sky." He was explicit in instructing his students to speak to everyone, not just some particular and chosen religious group.

In my translation there is no suggestion that readers should believe in anything, join an organization, or abandon their cherished religious and philosophical ideals. I see no reason why a Christian, an agnostic, a Buddhist, or even an atheist would not be charmed and inspired by the Gospels. Anyone can freely and without any worries read the Gospels and be enriched.

These texts are sacred not because they belong to a particular religion or spiritual tradition but because they offer a vision and a way of life that transcends the limits of reason and will. They show a figure in love with life and with a heart open to all sorts of people, but at the same time a figure constantly in tune with the Sky Father, that image of ultimate transcendence that provides an opening, a tear in the fabric of human consciousness, a doorway to the infinite and the eternal.

The Gospels are not just books of practical wisdom—how to live more effectively. They are also books of mysteries, assuming that to be fully human we have to open ourselves to the mysterious depth and height of the world that is our home.

Who Was Jesus?

It is a simple question, isn't it? Who was Jesus? But the debate over the historical Jesus has been raging for at least two centuries. There is not much factual material to go on, and though the Gospels often sound like biography or history, clearly they are largely stories told to evoke a religious milieu. Historically, they are full of contradictions and gaps and fantasy material. This does not make them worthless in themselves. On the contrary, they are marvelous, simply ingenious inventions for spiritual teaching, but as history they are unreliable, to say the least.

It appears that Jesus was born around 4 BCE, when Romans were occupying the Mediterranean area of Jesus's birth and travels. Herod the Great was king, having been put in place by the Romans. Greek language and culture were strong in the area, and Egypt, with its colorful past and rich spiritual culture, was not far away. There is evidence of a temple to the Greek god Dionysus in Jesus's area, and yet he was also dealing daily with Jewish teachings, customs, and rules. The Gospels portray many verbal skirmishes between Jesus and leaders, religious and social, who spoke up for Jewish law and tradition.

Jesus taught in the synagogues and to some appeared to be the long-awaited Messiah, the anointed leader of a new Jewish order. Many events and sayings in the Gospels echo Hebrew Bible writings, suggesting a layer of Messiah in Jesus's words and actions. But this aspect also casts a shadow on Jesus's presence and work, leading to the notion that he was "king of the Jews" and therefore a threat to Roman, local, and religious authority. Jesus was executed somewhere around 30 CE, perhaps in his early thirties.

It is often said that people who read the Gospels see the Jesus they want to see. Some understand him to be a religious reformer, some a social rebel, and some the founder of a religious tradition. He is sometimes described as a teacher of wisdom, a label that comes close to my own view but is not quite serious enough. I see him more as a social mystic, like a shaman who can heal and lead people to appreciate multiple layers of their reality.

At his baptism, the sky opens and the Sky Father speaks favorably of him, blessing him, essentially. For me, this is a key moment, because Jesus is forever talking about his Father in the sky, recommending that we always live in relation to that transcendent realm as well as in the present moment, where our goodwill and powers of healing are always needed.

Jesus also has a relationship to the dead, and his own death is always looming. So in the end we have a Jesus who as shaman and mystic speaks and acts from the plane of daily life, from the transcendent level of the Father, and in the realm of the dead. This is more than lessons in practical wisdom. It is a profound mystical vision that combines social action, based on the principle of friendship and not just altruism, and an all-embracing mystical awareness of timeless realities and sensibilities.

Some think that Jesus wanted to create a religion or a church. Some think he was often speaking about the afterlife. In my translation and commentary, I move in a different direction. I think he was trying to convince people to live in an entirely different way, with basic values of love and community instead of self-interest and conflict. He suggested keeping the highest ideals in mind instead of merely trying to amass money and possessions. He spoke and acted contrary to moralistic laws and customs and showed in his manner of living that friends and good company were worth more than pious activities. He told all his students to be healers and to help people rid themselves of compulsive behaviors. Above all, he suggested that we get over all the artificial boundaries set up between religions and cultures and live as though we were all brothers and sisters. "Who is my family?" (Matthew 12:48), he asks, and he points to the students and others gathered around him.

What Is a Gospel?

The story of Jesus's life and teachings was written down, after a fairly long period of oral storytelling, by many writers, each having a different purpose. We get the essentials of the story in Mark, strong references to Jewish tradition in Matthew, important elaboration of the stories and teachings in Luke, and a mystical dimension in John. By the fifth century CE, the church had made these four versions official. They are called "canonical," the only ones approved by the church at that time: Matthew, Mark, Luke, and John. These writings first appeared somewhere between 65 CE and 110 CE, at least thirty-five years after Jesus's death. The Book of Mark was the oldest, and the writers of Matthew and Luke took some material from Mark.

So think about that—a teacher appears and dies, and decades later a few devotees write down some stories about his life and try to capture his teachings, based on what had been passed down by word of mouth. Besides problems with memory, the various stories, as we see in the canonical Gospels, conveyed a different sense of what Jesus was all about. They were interpretations, not histories.

Two millennia later, modern people try to make sense of these written documents. Not being historians, they tend to take the stories as plain fact and even try to live by their interpretations. Some of the tales are quite fantastic: miraculous healings, raising the dead to life, the teacher himself surviving death, miraculous meals, and angels appearing here and there. Put together these two aspects—fantastic events and a tendency to take every word literally—and you have problems in understanding.

Strictly speaking, the word *gospel* in the original Greek means "good message." It has been translated as "good news" or "glad tidings," both accurate and beautiful phrases. But what is the good news? That is not so easy to sort out.

The Translation

If you have grown up reading the Gospels or hearing them read in church, you may think that the translation you take for granted is official or sacred. But the Gospels were originally written in a form of Greek spoken by people in everyday life. Historians generally agree that Jesus spoke Aramaic and that the Gospels were written in Greek. There is no widely accepted ancient Aramaic version, though some think that the Greek Gospels, in particular Matthew and Luke, may have been based on Aramaic sources.

If you were to read the Gospels in the original Greek, you would be surprised, maybe even shocked, to see how simple the language is. The vocabulary is limited, and many sentences read almost like a book meant for children. The Book of Luke is somewhat more sophisticated than Mark, and Matthew lies in the middle. But still the Greek is quite plain. This means that a translator has great liberty in using a number of different words for the simple ones that keep coming up and is likely to infuse his version with his own biases and points of view.

In rendering the Greek Gospels into English, I would like to have come up with astonishing, florid, and entrancing phrases. But, as I said, the original is so simple that it would be a travesty to make it too elaborate. I had two principles in mind as I made this translation: I wanted to give the reader a version that would flow gracefully and be as clear and limpid as I could make it, and I wanted to use striking new English words for a few key terms that I thought were usually misunderstood.[1] I worked hard to be sure that my versions of these words had the backing of history and scholarship.

Jesus as Poet

I see Jesus as a spiritual poet. There is a striking passage in the Book of Matthew where his students are being literal and he corrects them. Matthew comments, "He said nothing to the people that was not a parable" (Matthew 13:34). By *poet* I do not mean that he speaks or writes poetry, but that he uses narrative and imagery to get his rich ideas across. He does not speak like an academic or a theologian, defining his terms and setting out his ideas pedantically. He is part teacher and part entertainer, a spiritual leader and a bard, a shaman and an enchanter.

A spiritual poet uses language for its beauty and for the power of its imagery. He wants to give the listener or reader insight into life. A poet does not force an understanding of life or an ideology onto his listeners. His narratives and images are meant to deepen a person's view of life. Some topics disappear in highly rationalistic language, while a more imagistic approach better conveys the mysteries involved.

If Jesus says that he speaks in parables, we should have a good idea about what a parable is. People often think of a parable as a simple, moral teaching story. But scripture scholar Robert Funk says that a parable helps us "cross over" into the mysterious land that Jesus is trying to evoke for us, a kingdom in which life is radically different. Similarly, the renowned scholar John Dominic Crossan says that a parable "shatters our complacency" and pulls us out of the comfortable picture of life we have always lived by.

A parable is the opposite of a gentle teaching story. It confronts us, asking us to change our way of seeing things. It turns conventional ideas upside down. Its very point is to make us uncomfortable. In plain teaching in the Book of Matthew, Jesus says, "Love your enemies and speak well of those who criticize you. This way you can become sons of your Father in the sky. For he makes the sun rise on the bad and the good and rain on the just and the unjust" (Matthew 5:44–45).

For many, this teaching is just too radical. How many people show any love for those they consider enemies? Later he tells the parable of a woman who hid a small amount of yeast in a large pile of flour. That is what the Jesus kingdom is like. It is not overt, not even visible, and it is tiny. Yet it can change a life and alter the course of the world. If only a small portion of people in the world understood that somehow you have to love your enemies, we might not go on dividing ourselves into the good and the bad, and the Jesus vision would gain some traction.

Much of what is written in the Gospels is poetic in style, sometimes metaphorical and allegorical. You have to have a sharp and sophisticated appreciation for symbol and image or you might completely misread the text.

For example, Jesus heals a blind man. Is this a simple miraculous good deed or does it speak to a less literal blindness? Do we all fail to see life for what it is and have the wrong view of our place in the world? The Gospel writer himself speaks about this more poetic kind of blindness.

A Better Word for "Sin"

Many translations of the Gospels have a moralistic air. The translator may think of Christianity as a religion of dos and don'ts, and that point of view leads him to translate certain words with a heavy moral slant. Take the word *sin*, so often used in English versions. Many readers of the Gospels know that the word originally meant "off the mark." Yet we do not use the word *sin* that way. We mean that someone has done something so bad that it merits everlasting punishment.

As a child growing up in a devout Catholic family, I was always being told, "Don't do that. You'll go to hell." What if an adult had said to me, "There you go again. You're off the mark. You need to get your values straight." At least I would have had a chance to do better.

I do not translate the Greek word *hamartia* as "sin" or even "off the mark." I prefer the reflections of the pre-Christian philosopher Aristotle, who in his book on poetry and drama, *Poetics*, discusses the role of *hamartia* in tragedy. He says it refers to an action done out of ignorance that has tragic consequences.

When I was a child, I had a BB gun and shot some birds. I still feel remorse for doing such a thing. I needed to be taught the value of innocent animal life. My ignorance led me to actions I now regret. I would not say that I committed a sin, but that in my ignorance I made a mistake that today I mourn. I do not consider myself a horrible person and carry that guilt with me, but I understand that I have to keep learning and become more aware so I do not make worse mistakes.

With Aristotle's thoughtful explanation in mind, how would you translate *hamartia*? It is complicated. Maybe several words would be better than one. I tend to use the word *mistake*, but I know that alone it sounds too weak. Usually I qualify it according to the context in which it is used. I do not want to imply that *hamartia* is a simple, everyday misstep, but neither do I want to suggest high-minded moralistic judgment, which I do not pick up from the Gospels in Greek. So I often used the term *tragic mistake*.

I have seen many English translations of the Gospels that try to make the language more modern in style than the familiar, often archaic renditions. I appreciate many of these modern versions, but none interprets the Gospels the way I do. I have my own idea of what the Gospels are about, and my translation expresses that viewpoint. *Sin* is only one of many key words that affect the way we understand what Jesus was up to and what he taught. Not finding *sin* in this translation, I hope you read the Gospels without beating yourself up for having done wrong. I hope you see that Jesus was not moralistic but rather deeply concerned about the roots of self-serving and destructive behavior.

Some Key Images

For years in writing many books I have turned to Greek classical literature for insight, especially the great tragedies and comedies, the hymns to the gods and goddesses, and the mythological stories. In the Gospel translation, whenever I come across any connection between the Gospels and these classical sources I take note of the crossover and see if it offers any special insight. In some cases, the parallels are striking and in others subtle and hidden. In general, an awareness of earlier uses of Greek terms helps us understand better what is being said in the Gospels.

As a student of both religion and depth psychology, I have spent many years studying Greek polytheism. I have been amazed by the richness, complexity, and insightfulness of the ancient tales of the gods and goddesses. If you were to read some of the penetrating essays by my mentor James Hillman or the well-known mythologist Joseph Campbell, you would see how the old Greek stories help us gain insight into the patterns and dynamics of our everyday lives.

As I was poring over the Greek text of the Gospels, studying one key word after another, I discovered several instances in which a reference to one of the ancient Greek stories lay buried in the etymology or structure of the word.

The Kingdom of the Sky

The clearest example is the phrase "kingdom of heaven" or "our father who art in heaven." The Greek word usually translated as "heaven" is *ouranos*. The word could be taken as an ordinary term for the sky, but it is also the exact name for the sky-god of the Greeks, Ouranos, today usually spelled Uranus, like the planet.

When I read the words *kingdom of heaven* (*ouranos*), I am inclined to translate it as "kingdom of the sky." I will say more about this image later, but my point here is that the Greek version of the Gospels has layers, and, whether intended or not, deep themes peek through and enrich the stories and teachings.

The Kingdom

You get the sense in the Gospels that Jesus is an intimate and special son of the Sky Father. The kingdom he is creating on earth is a way of life sanctioned by this Father. When asked how to pray, Jesus says, "Say, our Father in the sky, may your name be held sacred...."

I see the sky as a metaphor, or better yet, an archetypal image. Its meaning is based on ordinary experience: You look at the sky at night or even during the day, and you may wonder about the meaning of everything and your place in life. You may imagine other worlds, other planets, and other civilizations. You may look into the light-blue daytime heavens or the blue-black night and sense infinity and eternity. The kingdom of the sky, therefore, is not like practical, factual, and self-absorbed life. It is an alternative, the object of wonder and perfection, eternal and infinite. The "Father" of that realm offers a more perfected idea of what human life could be.

The kingdom of the sky comprises those people who live the values Jesus specifies in his teaching, especially the one about respecting any person who is not of your circle. Jesus does not talk about love as a sentimental emotion. That is why I usually translate *agape* as "respect." If your basic motivation in all of life is love and respect, you are automatically in the kingdom. But take note: Jesus makes it clear that your actions have to follow your values in this regard.

The Sky and the Sky Father

I prefer to use the word *sky* instead of *heaven* because it is a concrete image. I do not mean a literal father in the clouds but rather the sky as an image for spirit. As I have read the passages about the Sky Father, I have had in mind the Native American mystic Black Elk, praying to the parents and grandparents in the sky.

Here is a typical passage from Black Elk that influenced me in translating *ouranos*:

> The fifth Grandfather spoke, the oldest of them all, the Spirit of the Sky. "My boy," he said, "I have sent for you and you have come. My power you shall see!" He stretched his arms and turned into a spotted eagle hovering. "Behold," he said, "all the wings of the air shall come to you, and they and the winds and the stars shall be like relatives. You shall go across the earth with my power." Then the eagle soared above my head and fluttered there; and suddenly the sky was full of friendly wings all coming toward me.[2]

This passage has much in common with the Gospels, as when Jesus is baptized and the Father speaks from the sky and the spirit appears as a hovering dove. The Gospel describes the sky as sometimes full of not wings but angels—close.

Hesiod, one of the early Greek spiritual poets, describes *ouranos*—the word used every time for Gospel phrases like "kingdom of the sky" and "our father in the heavens"—this way:

> *The first one born of Gaia (Earth) was Ouranos.*
> *He was as big as she was.*
> *He was the sky full of stars.*
> *He spread over her*
> *and was*
> *a solid ground for the holy immortals.*

You can pray to the Father, as Jesus did, and yet know that you are addressing something mysterious and vastly spiritual. Our usual anthropomorphic—humanlike—language is only an approximation of the sublime mystery of this Father. As the spirit of the sky, he is the "ground for the holy immortals" or, we might say, "the ground for our spiritual vision."

The kingdom of the sky or the heavens is a place set apart because of its special values and the primacy of its rule of love and respect, agape. Jesus wants neither the rule-bound religion of the church officials nor the self-satisfied realm of the purely secular. He calls for a third alternative, a place where you can live a life based on spiritual values of love and respect.

The Commentary

Because there are so many words of such complexity in the Gospels, I have included many notes on the translation and comments on the meaning. Some of them come from other sources, offering either an expert reflection on the passage or special insight from an artist. From the beginning, I wanted to include comments from thinkers of many different spiritual traditions. Why not? Their different perspectives open up fresh ways of understanding the Gospel stories and teachings. I try to set aside my own academic interests and get to the heart of the matter. If I mention an expert or a writer from history, such as Aristotle's thoughts about mistakes, or a poet such as Anne Sexton, I do not call on them as authorities, as though I were writing a school paper. I mention them because their brilliant ideas are relevant. I hope that their way of seeing the issue will enrich your reading of the Gospels.

Most of the time my comments are my own take on the passage in question. A friend advised me on this project: "People aren't going to read your version because you're a scholar or have a mind-blowing translation to offer. They'll want to know what you think about the various stories and teachings. They want to know your ideas because you write about the soul and how to live more deeply and with less conflict." I heard what he said and beefed up my own commentary.

I want to open up the Gospel message by showing how people of various traditions and expertise interpreted certain passages. I quote Christian, Jewish, Sufi, Buddhist, and secular writers; poets, politicians, theologians, and Bible experts. Then I bring my own point of view to various passages, basing my reflections on my studies in depth psychology, world religions, mythology, and the arts. I rely on decades of experience as a psychotherapist, and I am aware of my own development in relation to the Gospels, from my childhood, when I heard them naively; to my monastic days, when I studied them in a Christian context; to now, when I blend the sacred and secular in everything I do and when I am always the psychotherapist. I could make a case that Jesus was a psychotherapist, and, in fact, the word *therapy* is often used in the Greek version to denote Jesus as a healer.

I think that the deeper point of the Gospels has been lost over the years, when people have focused on them as a source of strict moral lessons and the cornerstones for belief, and the establishment of a religion, church, or spiritual community. To me, Jesus says clearly that he is speaking to everyone who will listen, and his message has sophisticated psychological insight. My intention with the commentary is to release the Gospels from their narrow confinements and show how valuable they are today to anyone at all looking for insight into how to live deeply and lovingly.

The Gospels Are for Everyone

Returning to a close study of the Gospels has helped me personally with my spiritual life. These texts now inspire me more forcefully than at any time in my life. I do not see them as representing or advocating a particular religious viewpoint but as setting out a way of life, a secular set of values, that could help humanity survive and thrive. While I certainly do not want to convert anyone to a particular religion or church, I would like to see the whole world adopt this vision for humanity, based on love, respect, healing, and compassion.

I hope this new translation will move us in a more thoughtful, subtle, and compassionate direction in our own way of living and in our attitude toward others, especially those different from us. This is a key part of Jesus's teachings: He is forever telling people to love those who are outside their own circle. The kingdom is for them, he says, not for the in crowd.

My own practice is to keep at hand several different translations of sacred texts. I have seven versions of the Tao Te Ching on my shelves close at hand. I recommend doing the same with the Gospels. For example, I have relied on the beautiful translation by the Jesus Seminar in a book called *The Acts of Jesus*. I respect the scholarship behind that translation, though I did not want to use such complicated language in my own version. I admire the witty and profound translations of certain passages by John Dominic Crossan in his book *The Essential Jesus*. "The somebodies will be nobodies and the nobodies will be somebodies." You cannot get a better translation than that.

If you are looking for a more extravagant version or something completely different, those translations are available. But if you want an accurate version that is close to the original in vocabulary and tone, presented in simple, rhythmic English, then mine might do. If you want help understanding the sometimes difficult passages, not from a scholar's point of view but from someone with a background in depth psychology, literature, and world religions, then you may want to add this one to your collection.

It is my conviction that the less literally you take most passages, the more you will be inspired to live an altogether different kind of life, one in which your heart is more open than you ever thought it could be. You will have found a kind of utopia, an island of meaning radically different from the one that rules the world today. You can live this way now and find joy and substance in your life. And you can promote it as a way for the future—not a belief system or a church or religion, but a way of being in the world, open and radically accepting.

Introduction to the Book of John

The Book of John begins with the dramatic words, "To begin, there was the Logos." *Logos* can mean "word," but in history it is a big concept, like dharma and Tao. It refers to the fact that the universe is not random but has order and meaning, and that a human being can grasp that meaning. From its opening words to its compassionate conclusion, the Book of John continually emphasizes Jesus's teachings as revealing the secrets of life and how to live in tune with them.

If you live in accord with the life and teachings of Jesus the Logos ("son of God" in the narrative of the Gospel), you are a child of God, one with the universe. You no longer struggle against yourself and against the world. I define *neurosis*, which is not only a psychological problem but also a matter of meaning and values, as not being aligned with the law of your particular destiny and nature, your own personal Logos. In this way, Jesus is a therapist. Throughout John, Jesus tells you how he can reset your lifestyle so it fulfills who you are instead of blocking your efforts.

In John's chapter 14 Jesus says, in the usual translation, "I am the way, the truth, and the life." The Greek word typically translated as "truth" is *aletheia*, rooted in Lethe, the river of forgetfulness. *A* in Greek means "not." So the Greek word for *truth* means "not forgetting." This does not refer to everyday forgetting but to forgetting what life is about and what your role is—a deep and essential forgetting. Marcel Detienne, an eminent scholar of Greek religion, defines *lethe* as "forgetfulness of the eternal truths." Therefore *aletheia* means remembering the eternal truths, the profound essentials of life. So I translate John 14:6 as "I am the path, the deep remembering, and the life." You can see that even here the main theme is strong: Jesus offers a path to profound fulfillment by calling to mind the eternal truths set by the Father. His life and teachings, his role as Logos and son of God, show us what the Father's will is.

John's Gospel Is Unique

The Book of John was written over the years 90–110 CE. Some experts think that it may have had several editors over that time and yet it has a stylistic unity. Chapter 21 was added at a late stage and perhaps chapters 15 through 17 as well. I treat the text as a whole, as given.

Unique to John is a vivid depiction of life above and life below, the Father in the sky, figuratively speaking, and the values of the sky, or heavens, embodied in the fully human life of Jesus. R. Alan Culpepper, a scholar known for his influential study of the literary qualities of John's Gospel, makes a key point: "The affective power of the narrative is the most important feature of its plot. By showing Jesus confronting a wide variety of individuals in every-day situations, the gospel dramatizes the message that the Word has become flesh and dwelt among us."[1]

I, too, think that the prologue is the key to grasping the full meaning of the Gospel. Keep in mind that Jesus is the Logos manifested in human form, not just in a mystical way but also insofar as his teachings are all about living a meaningful life. Many different stories and episodes in the Gospel repeat this steady theme, including the raising of Lazarus, an image for waking up to the Logos instead of remaining asleep and unaware of how to live.

The other three Gospels emphasize the image of the new life as a kingdom, not of this world but of the sky. It is a utopian realm in which old values of self-interest and violence give way to love and neighborliness. In John we find a shift of emphasis and a different image. John frequently uses images of water and other fluids: baptism, water to wine, spit and mud for healing, water and blood from Jesus's side, Nicodemus and birth from water and spirit. In each case we see the two realms of spirit and the natural world linked. Our job is to be spiritual and naturally human at every moment, the deepest secret revealed in this Gospel.

With two exceptions—the conversations with Nicodemus and with Pilate, where Jesus refers to the kingdom of God—generally in John you do not enter a new kind of kingdom. Instead, you are intimately aligned with the archetypal Father, the paternal nature of reality, the laws of life and way of unforgetfulness. You do not forget your Father and his expectations, nor do you betray them. John's Gospel has several examples of betrayal—Peter, Judas,

Pilate, and the Jewish authorities—showing that it is not always easy to be on the Father's path.

Also unique to John, the miracles in this Gospel function as "signs," as he says, and are fewer but no less dramatic than in the other Gospels. John does not seem as interested in astonishing his readers as in showing how life lived according to Jesus's teachings is wondrous and meaningful in itself.

The Structure of John's Gospel

John is structured like a musical composition. It is not one logical, linear narrative but rather a blend of forms and motifs that come and go like themes in a long piece of music:

> *Meaningful miracles:* water becoming wine, knowledge of the Samaritan woman's life story, healing an official's son, the Pool of Bethesda, 153 fish caught, raising Lazarus.

> *A series of "I am" statements:* "I am the light of the cosmos" (the world is no longer dark and unconscious), "I am the good shepherd," "I am the real vine" (a way of connecting to the source of vitality), "Before Abraham was born, I am" (the teaching of Jesus is timeless), "I am the bread of life" (considering, digesting, and living out Jesus's teachings satisfies the hunger for life, the wish for more, and the need for spiritual nurturance).

> *Suspicion and threats:* The suspicion of the Jewish authorities and the frequent threats of arrest.

> *Lessons in humility and respect:* Mary of Bethany oils Jesus's feet, Jesus washes his students' feet.

> *Dramatic scenes with complicated characters:* torture, crucifixion, and resurrection.

It is a richly textured story, artful in its organization and inspiring to read. The key is to keep the Logos in mind. Jesus reveals how life is put together and how it is to be lived. The full story tells you that when you live this way you may be misunderstood and persecuted. But ultimately you have overcome the dangers of unconsciousness and a lost soul.

Colorful, Archetypal Characters

Archetypal means "profoundly and essentially human." John presents us with striking personalities that point to persons in us. For example, for centuries people have identified with Martha and Mary, two valid ways of being in the world. We feel compassion for the Samaritan woman at the well who mirrors our own failure to live a perfect life. We identify with "doubting Thomas," who represents a basic human difficulty with faith and trust.

This Gospel is full of colorful, complex characters unique to John, beginning with a key figure, Nathanael, who is mentioned only briefly. It is he who says, "What good can come out of Nazareth?" (John 1:46). How can the Logos, who was there at creation, come from a small and insignificant town? Yet it is Nathanael who also says, "Rabbi, you are the son of God. You are the King of Israel" (John 1:49). This relatively minor character expresses his skepticism and yet recognizes the fullness of who Jesus is.

Nicodemus is a fascinating character as well. He wants to learn the teaching, but his tendency toward literalism gets in the way. To be reborn, do you have to crawl back into the womb? Yet people read the Gospels every day with a similar failure of insight and appreciation for metaphor.

The Samaritan woman at the well is another richly portrayed figure. You can feel her struggle as she tries to make sense of her life; she wants badly to feel alive. She is interested in what Jesus has to offer—living water.

In John, Mary and Martha, who also appear in the Book of Luke, represent followers who are strong in their faith in Jesus and also connected to him with a deep love. Martha immediately goes out to meet Jesus before he arrives at her home, while Mary stays inside. Then Mary takes over and tells Jesus of her faith in his power to transform death to life. They are two strong, loving women who, as close followers, say something about Jesus's powers and the depth of his feeling. Once again we see the spiritual and the human working together in him.

The dark tone enters with "the Jews." They, too, have a problem with literalism, understanding Jesus's kingdom to be political and his philosophy a threat to their religious tradition.

Finally, there is the mysterious "beloved disciple," the one who leans on Jesus's chest at the Last Supper and who is entrusted to Jesus's mother on

Golgotha. Many commentators believe this person was John the Apostle and writer of the Gospel. Or maybe he was Jesus's brother James, or Lazarus, whom Jesus loved. Or was it Mary of Magdala? We don't know, but the mystery just adds to the emotional pulse of the story.

One Theme, Many Stories

The stories in John are not brief and simple parables but long, complex, layered, and symbolic narratives highlighting various aspects of the central theme. Water changed into wine symbolizes the change needed in us to follow Jesus. We need to go from plain living and concern about being pure to vivid, empathic people intoxicated with Jesus's vision. We also need to get over our blindness, our failure to see the Logos in ordinary life. We need to rise out of our unconsciousness and deadness, resurrect into the fullness of who we are.

The Jesus of John's Gospel is both human and mythic: "The Logos took flesh and lived with us" (John 1:14). Logos has become a human being. But as the distinguished scholar George W. E. Nickelsburg says of Jesus, "He knows who Nathanael is, though he never met him. He knows how many husbands the Samaritan woman has. In Gethsemane, there is no agony."[2] Jesus lives as one of us, but at the same time he is always a pointer to the very nature of things, human and superhuman.

The best way to read this Gospel is first to come to terms with its mystical language of Logos and Father. This is the high level, spiritual and exalted, taking you far in your imagination. I have offered some hints about making this dimension real and tangible. The next step is to notice how Jesus embodies human life: his compassion, his capacity for friendship, his love of life, his sensuality. The earthly Jesus appears early on in the enchanting story of the wedding party at Cana and continues in the anecdote of Mary of Bethany rubbing oil on his feet. The Gospel concludes with warm stories of a resurrected Jesus.

In this Gospel, Thomas, Peter, Mary, and Jesus's students as a whole often struggle to understand the multilayered comments he makes about his Father and the spiritual meaning of his words. The modern reader has a similar challenge: getting ordinary worldly life and the spiritual order both distinct and connected. In this Gospel Jesus is both Logos and chef. He constantly speaks about his Father, and yet he calls himself the "bread of life," and he cooks fish for his friends. He models how to be fully in this life with its deep pleasures of friendship and dining and, at the same time, focused on and devoted to a spiritual life based on the principle of love.

Personally, I am glad that John comes last in the usual arrangement of Gospels. It gives us a different viewpoint and emphasis. It boldly speaks of how the pure spiritual realm intersects with the ordinary human plane. It presents a deeply loving, feeling, and sometimes emotionally tortured Jesus, who is nonetheless the son of the starkly spiritual Father, and always connected to him and revealing his purposes. John's style is unique and its main message has a direct force. As a piece of literature and as a spiritual guide it is enchanting, inspiring, and beautiful.

THE BOOK OF
JOHN

1   *Logos* means much more than "word," the usual English translation. *Logos* can mean "word," "story," "myth," "mystery," "plan," "teaching," or "logic." It would not be misleading to say, "To begin there was the logic." I would rather keep the Greek word and imagine all the meanings as valid. "Begin" is also narrow, but it has the advantage of echoing the opening of Genesis. The word is *arche*, as in archetypal. It could mean the state of origins or the originating stuff of life.

2   Compare a line from the creation story of the Huitoto of Columbia: "Awonawilona conceived within himself and thought outward in space, whereby mists of increase, streams potent of growth, were evolved and uplifted" (Sanders and Peek).

3   Whatever you say is LOGOS,
    ocean-fountain
    pearl-hoard
    incisive proof
    of the Intellect
    whose cutting edge
    is but the blade of the tongue
    which reveals the hidden fires
    which sear the universe
    with the heart's candle flame.
    —"On the Logos," in *The Drunken Universe: An Anthology of Persian Sufi Poetry*, trans. Peter Lamborn Wilson and Nasrollah Pourjavady (Grand Rapids: Phanes Press, 1987), 15

4   This light is related to the emptiness (sunyata) notion of Eastern religions, expressed beautifully in the language of improvisation by theologian Gabriel Vahanian: "In the Gospel of John, the incarnation means the constantly unique event through which destiny is improvised once and for all and not its objectification. Human existence, because it can never be rehearsed, is not an institution but a necessary improvisation of destiny. Admittedly, institutions too are born of the necessity of improvisation, but they freeze it, they codify it, just as dogmas and religion betray faith by codifying the acts of faith—through which they are improvised—forgetting that existence itself, as a spontaneous act of faith, is an impertinent improvisation on the theme of God's reality, of the presentness of God" (Vahanian).

Chapter 1

*T*o begin,
       there was the Logos. [1]
And the Logos was
       close to God.
The Logos
       was God
              and was in the predawn with God. [2]
From it
       everything came into being,
Without it
       nothing that exists would have come to be.
In it
       was life. [3]
A life
       that was humanity's light,
a light
       aglow in a darkness
              that doesn't darken it. [4]

5 Do not overlook this significant phrase, "a child of God." Such a being is one who does not live only by worldly norms and expectations but whose sight is always on the infinite, utopia, and the mysterious possibilities for a different life.

6 "The body to be realized is the body of the cosmic man, the body of the universe as one perfect man. The word that is incarnate in Christ is the word that is incarnate in the universe by the creative fiat; it is the logos of the universe now recapitulated in the divine-human body."
　　—Norman O. Brown, *Love's Body* (Berkeley: University of California Press, 1966), 226

7 The word usually translated as "truth" is *aletheia*. But the renowned scholar Marcel Detienne translates it as a traditional ancient poet's kind of remembering. "For the poet, remembrance (*aletheia*) came through a personal vision that ensured direct access to the events his memory evoked. His privilege was to enter into contact with the other world, and his memory granted him the power to decipher the invisible" (Detienne). The poet is the master of truth (*aletheia*) by recalling the ancient mythic teachings.

A man sent from God, John, came to witness, to testify about the light, so that through him everyone could have faith. He was not the light but came as a witness to the light. This was a profound light that comes into the world and illuminates everyone. It is cosmic. Through it the cosmos came to be. But the world didn't see it for what it was.

He came to his own people, and they didn't accept him. He gave whoever did accept him the opportunity to become a child of God,[5] one who trusts in his name, who is born not just in the ways of the flesh or in a human sense, but in God.

> *The Logos took flesh*
>   *and lived with us.*[6]
> *We saw*
>   *and appreciated*
>   *his brilliance,*
> *the brilliance*
>   *of one who is*
>   *the only child*
>   *of the Father,*
> *full of grace*
>   *and deep remembrance.*[7]

8 *Pleroma* becomes an important word in later reflection on Jesus. Both Paul
   and Gnostic writers spoke of the pleroma as the fullness of being before the
   world is differentiated. More concretely, we might think of Jesus's vast and
   profound imagination of what human life could be as his fullness, while from
   it we can create our lives.

9 This is an extraordinary statement, worth close study and meditation. No
   one has seen God, but as you get to know Jesus in his teaching and example,
   you will, in a sense, see God. You will get over your blindness, a frequent
   theme in the Gospels that does not have to be taken literally.

10 "Who are you?" is an important question. It is difficult to know who a real
   prophet is, in the sense of one speaking for the divine, the infinite and sublime values. There is so much ego and personality disorder surrounding the
   spiritual that you have to ask always, "Who are you?" Is the person we hope
   to follow truly making a good path to the infinite?

11 Isaiah 40:3

12 It is even difficult to recognize a real prophet when you see one. He or she
   may not look like someone who speaks for the Divine. There may be no
   clear and obvious signals. You have to look closely for the right signs.

13 "Jesus Christ immolates the age of war in the only way possible: by sacrific-
   ing himself as the Ram or Lamb of God. In doing so he ushers in the Age
   of Pisces (second-first millennia AD), the era which cherishes in its heart an
   ideal of devotion and love."
   —Joscelyn Godwin, *Mystery Religions in the Ancient World* (San Francisco: Harper
   & Row, 1981), 99

John acknowledged him and said publicly, "This is who I referred to when I said, 'Though he comes after me, he is more important than me, because he is above me.' Out of his fullness, his pleroma,[8] we have received everything, one gift after another. Just as we received the law from Moses, we have received grace and meaning from Jesus Christos.

No one has ever seen God, but the only child of God, who enjoys the embrace of the Father, showed him to us.[9]

When the Jews sent priests and Levites from Jerusalem to him to ask who he was, this is what John said. He confessed it and never retracted it, "I am not Christos."

They asked him, "All right, then. Are you Elijah?"

"No, I'm not."

"Are you the prophet?"

"No," he said.

So they went on.

"Who are you?[10] We have to give an answer to the people who sent us. What do you have to say about yourself?"

He said, "I am a voice of someone crying out in the wilderness, 'making a good path for the master,' as the prophet Isaiah said."[11]

The Pharisees had sent their people on a mission, so they asked again. "If you're not Christos, not Elijah, and not the prophet, why are you baptizing?"

John responded, "I baptize with water, but there is someone out there among you who you don't recognize.[12] He will come after me. I'm not worthy enough to loosen his sandal."

All this took place in Bethany, beyond the Jordan, where John was baptizing.

The very next day he saw Jesus coming up to him and said, "This is the lamb[13] of God who pardons the world's wrongdoing. This is the one I spoke about when I said, 'Someone is coming after me who is more important than me, because he's above me.' I didn't know him. I baptized with water precisely so that he would become known to Israel."

14 "Maybe my mother was a greater theologian than I realized. When she told
me to become the Messiah, I thought she meant I should enter rabbinic
school. I had no idea she meant that every one of us already is. You are the
Messiah. You already have everything you need, and you are where you
need to be."
   —Lawrence Kushner, *Eyes Remade for Wonder: A Lawrence Kushner Reader*
   (Woodstock, VT: Jewish Lights Publishing, 1998), 208

15 This is a good question in general. Can we glimpse the Logos in an ordinary
person? Someone in our own neighborhood? Is there a connection between
the ordinary human and the eternal Logos? Jesus seems to be always asking
us ordinary people to let the light of human excellence shine in us.

John testified further, "I saw the spirit coming down from the sky as a dove, hovering over him. I didn't recognize him, but the one who sent me to baptize with water said to me, 'The one on whom you see the spirit coming down and hovering, this is the one who baptizes in the holy spirit.' I have seen and have testified that this is the son of God."

The next day John was standing with two of his followers when he saw Jesus walking by. He said, "Look, the lamb of God." The two followers heard him say that and followed Jesus. Jesus turned around and saw them following and said, "What are you looking for?"

They said, "Rabbi, Teacher, where do you live?"

He said, "Come and see."

So they went and saw where he was living and stayed with him that day, since it was already the tenth hour, late afternoon. One of the two who heard John speak and followed Jesus was Andrew, Simon Peter's brother. He found his own brother Simon and told him, "We have found the Messiah, Christos." He brought him to Jesus.[14]

Jesus looked at him and said, "You're Simon, the son of John. We'll call you Cephas, or Peter."

The next day Jesus suggested they go into Galilee, where he found Philip. Jesus said to him, "Follow me." Philip was from Bethsaida, Andrew and Peter's town. Philip found Nathanael and told him, "We've met the one that Moses in the law and the prophets wrote about—Jesus of Nazareth, Joseph's son."

Nathanael said, "What good can come out of Nazareth?"[15]

Philip said, "Well, come and see."

Jesus saw Nathanael coming toward him and said, "Look, an Israelite in whom there is no artifice."

Nathanael said, "How do you know me?"

16 According to an old philosophical dictum, "To be is to be perceived." Jesus
perceives Nathanael, who then recognizes the divinity in Jesus. So the dictum is extended to: "To be is to be perceived is to perceive." This power
of perception, associated with the apostle Nathanael, returns at the end of
John's Gospel, where Nathanael is among those fishing who recognize Jesus
standing on the shore. Jesus cooks their fish, adds some bread, and gives
them breakfast.

Jesus replied, "Before Philip called you, when you were standing under a fig tree, I noticed you."[16]

Nathanael said, "Rabbi, you are the son of God. You are the king of Israel."

Jesus said, "Because I told you that I saw you under the fig tree you trust me? You'll see greater things. I can tell you now, you will see the sky open up and angels of God going up and down around the son of man."

1   Jesus's hesitation and the active presence of his mother allows a deep femi-
    nine soul factor into the equation. Jungian psychology would say that the
    anima overcomes other concerns and urges toward a mysterious contribu-
    tion to a wedding. Jung wrote often about the sacred and inner marriage that
    is part of everyone's process in becoming a full person. The story of Cana
    teems with implications and depths.

2   This is a clear instruction to take this story as symbolic and as a source of
    insight into Jesus's very nature and what he was doing. According to the bib-
    lical scholar Marcus J. Borg, this story "is about a wedding banquet at which
    the wine never runs out, and the best is saved for last. The story of the wed-
    ding at Cana invites us to see that the story of Jesus is about *this*" (Borg).

Chapter 2

On the third day there was a wedding in Cana of Galilee, and Jesus's mother was there. Jesus and his followers had been invited. The wine ran out and Jesus's mother said to him, "They're out of wine."

Jesus said to her, "Dear woman, what does that have to do with you and me? My time has not yet come."[1]

His mother told the waiters, "Do whatever he tells you."

There were six stone water jars set out for the Jewish ritual of purification. Each contained twenty or thirty gallons. Jesus told them, "Fill the jars with water." So they filled them up to the brim. Then he said, "Pour some out now and take it to the wedding planner." So they took it to him.

When the wedding planner had tasted the water that had become wine, he called the groom. He didn't know where the wine had come from, though the waiters knew because they had poured it out. He told the groom, "Most people serve the good wine first, and then when people have had a lot to drink, they serve the less expensive varieties. But you kept the excellent wine until now."

This event in Cana of Galilee was the first of Jesus's symbolic acts that revealed who he was.[2] His followers developed trust in him.

3 The early theologian Origen (185–254) as usual has a poetic interpretation: "The temple is the soul equipped with reason. Jesus applies his discipline to it, when it has senseless, earthly and dangerous qualities. It appears to be beautiful but isn't. Jesus drives these things out with his words woven from teachings that give example and warning, so that the soul will follow heavenly and spiritual laws" (Origen).

4 Psalm 69:9

After this they went to Capernaum—he, his mother and brothers, and his followers. They stayed there for a few days.

The Jewish Passover was approaching, so Jesus went on to Jerusalem. There, in the temple, he found people selling oxen, sheep, and doves, and clerks were sitting at tables dealing with money. He made a whip out of cords and drove them out of the temple, along with their sheep and oxen. Then he overturned the money tables and scattered the coins of the clerks. To the ones selling doves he said, "Get rid of this stuff. Stop making my Father's house a bazaar."[3]

His followers recalled that it had been written, "A passion for your house will eat me up."[4]

The Jews said to him, "Can you give us any proof that you have the authority to do such things?"

Jesus said, "Tear down this temple and in three days I'll raise it up."

The Jews said, "It took forty-six years to build this temple, and you'll resurrect it in three days?"

He was, in fact, talking about the temple of his body. Later, after he was raised from the dead, his followers recalled that he had said this, and they believed the scripture and the words Jesus had spoken.

When he was in Jerusalem for Passover at the time of the festival, many put their trust in his name and saw the extraordinary things he was doing. For his part, Jesus didn't confide in anyone. He knew human beings. He didn't need anyone to tell him about people because he knew what people are made of.

1   This word in Greek can mean either "again" or "above." I prefer "above"
    because throughout the Gospels the kingdom is connected to the sky, the
    heavens, or the "highest." It is as though there are two levels of existence: a
    lower one that is unconscious, something like the Eastern idea of samsara,
    and a more subtle and aware dimension, where communal values of justice,
    friendship, and love are the defining principles. We are all born into physi-
    cal, material life and then have an opportunity for another birth into the
    realm of the kingdom.

2   "Jewish tradition holds that 'living water' is the only kind suitable for puri-
    fication. This is water connected to a larger source, such as a stream or the
    ocean.... On a symbolic level, it indicates that the psyche is dead unless it
    maintains a constant connection with the deeper streams of universal life."
        —Richard Smoley, *Inner Christianity: A Guide to the Esoteric Tradition* (Boston:
        Shambhala, 2002), 213

3   Here the above point is quite clear. If you are born of the flesh, you will have
    a material existence. If you are born of the spirit, as well, you will have a
    spiritual existence, too.

4   People who are awake do not look different. You must listen closely to them
    to sense how they embody the kingdom. You hear the wind, almost like
    music. You sense the kingdom, almost like subtle, poetic resonance.

O Great Spirit,
whose voice I hear in the winds
and whose breath gives life to all the world,
hear me.
I am small and weak.
I need your strength and wisdom.
    —Chief Yellow Lark, in *God Makes the Rivers to Flow: An Anthology of the World's
    Sacred Poetry and Prose*, ed. Ecknath Easwaran (Tomales, CA: Nilgiri Press,
    2003), 188

Chapter 3

Aman among the Pharisees named Nicodemus was a leader among the Jews. One night he visited Jesus and said, "Rabbi, we know that you are a teacher who comes from God. No one could do the remarkable things you do unless God was with him."

Jesus responded, "I tell you honestly that unless a person is born from above[1] he can't really see the kingdom of God."

Nicodemus said, "How can a person be born when he's old? He can't go back into his mother's womb and be born again, can he?"

Jesus said, "I'm speaking honestly to you. Unless a person is born of both water[2] and spirit he can't be part of the kingdom of God. What is born of the flesh is flesh, and of the spirit, spirit.[3]

"Don't be shocked when I say you have to be born a second time. The wind blows wherever it wants to. You hear its sound, but you don't know where it came from and where it's going. Anyone born of the spirit is like that, too."[4]

Nicodemus said, "How is this possible?"

Jesus said, "You're a teacher in Israel and you don't understand this?"

"Yes, but we talk about what we know and what we can see. You don't seem to appreciate our reasoning."

5   Numbers 21:8

6   "The kingdom is in the thoughtless zone. To live in the thoughtless zone
    is the same as to live in the timeless zone.... Eternity is not the indefinite
    extension of time; it is the disappearance of time."
        —Kenneth S. Leong, *The Zen Teachings of Jesus* (New York: Crossroad, 2001), 75

7   "The Essenes were a Jewish sect that had broken with the official Judaism of
    the Jerusalem temple and had withdrawn to the desert at the Wadi Qumran.
    They understood their situation in terms of the antithesis of light and dark-
    ness, truth and lie, a dualism that ultimately went back to Persian dualism—
    and then moved forward toward Gnosticism."
        —James M. Robinson, *The Nag Hammadi Library in English* (San Francisco:
        HarperSanFrancisco, 1990), 7

"If I talk about earthly matters and you don't believe me, how will you believe me if I talk about spiritual things? No one has gone up skyward except one who came down from the sky—the son of man. Just as Moses lifted up a snake in the wilderness, so the son of man has to be lifted up, so that anyone who trusts in him will have unending life.⁵ God loved the world so much that he gave his only son. Whoever trusts in him will not be nullified but will enjoy eternity in life.⁶

"God didn't send the son into the world to judge it, but to save it. If you trust in him, you won't be judged. If you don't trust in him, you're already judged, because you don't trust in the name of the only son of God.

"This is how people are sorted out: The light has come into the world, but some people love darkness rather than light— their actions are not good.⁷ Anyone who detests the light doesn't come to the light because his actions will be shown for what they are. But whoever practices what is deep and true moves close to the light. It's clear that his actions originate in God."

After this, Jesus and his followers went to the land of Judea. There Jesus spent time with them and baptized. John, too, was baptizing in Aenon near Salim because of all the water there. People were coming to him and being baptized before John was put in prison.

An argument arose between John's followers and a Jew about purification. They approached John and said, "Rabbi, that man who was with you on the other side of the Jordan, the one you talked about, is baptizing and all the people are going to him."

8   The bride here is the deep truth of Jesus's point of view.

9   This is a beautiful expression of genuine humility. We are all like the friend of the groom, not the groom himself. Our joy comes not from our accomplishments but from living the beautiful life Jesus sets out for us, a life of neighborliness, peaceful intentions, and unexpected love.

10 Here we see the two planes laid out clearly—the earthly and the spiritual. Distinguishing them does not necessarily create a divided experience. The two overlap, but the values of each are very different. This Gospel will expand on this theme as it goes on.

11 "Eternal life … is not 'life after death' but the dimension of eternity that abides in our mortal life. We are called to awaken to this Life before we die, just as Christ did."
      —Jean-Yves Leloup, *The Gospel of Philip: Jesus, Mary Magdalene, the Gnosis of Sacred Union*, trans. Joseph Rowe (Rochester, VT: Inner Traditions, 2004), 16

The Renaissance philosopher Marsilio Ficino says that the soul "is partly in time and partly in eternity." We live our temporal lives and yet have a major element that is timeless. Here the Gospel is describing a path to that timeless dimension.

John responded, "A person gets nothing unless it has been granted to him from above. You know that I said, 'I am not Christos' and 'I have been sent ahead.' Whoever has the bride[8] is the groom, but the friend of the groom, standing by and listening to him, is very happy because of the groom's voice.[9] My joy, too, is complete. He must increase, and I must decrease. One who comes from above is above everyone. One who is of the earth is from the earth and talks like an earth being. The one who comes from above is above everyone.[10]

"One who comes from above describes what he has heard and seen, and yet rarely does anyone accept his report. Still, whoever accepts what he says grants that God is truthful. The one who God has sent speaks God's words and offers spirit without limit. The Father loves the son and has given him everything, and so whoever trusts in the son has eternity in life.[11] Whoever doesn't follow the son will never feel alive but will sense God's anger directed at him."

1   Sometimes the waters of life take the image-form of a river or stream, such as the Jordan River in which Jesus was baptized. Life flows, and it is important to be in that flow. But here the image is a well, indicating that the same water of life can be found in our depths, deep within the crust of earth on which we live. The woman comes to the well for plain water, but Jesus has the deep water of life to offer.

2   This is a fascinating and complex story. We begin with an old theme: Jesus is concerned with people who are usually rejected. He simply goes against the spirit of his times and offers his teaching to the Samaritan woman. To make the story more interesting, the image of a well and its water is central. The teaching is a life-giving water, a metaphor that Jesus himself draws out. He speaks of the substance as an alchemist might, not as literal water but an image for the qualities of water that the teaching has. Later, alchemy would speak of *aqua permanens*, eternal water, that can contribute significantly to the process of becoming a person with a soul.

   The story also brings in Jacob from the Book of Genesis, who meets his wife Rachel at a well for watering sheep. Jacob is one of the great patriarchs of Judaism, whose name was changed to Israel.

   We might also notice that Jesus engages the Samaritan woman, even though at that time a man was not supposed to talk to a woman in public.

Chapter 4

When Jesus learned that the Pharisees heard he was getting more followers and baptizing more people than John—actually it was Jesus's followers who were doing the baptisms—he left Judea and went back to Galilee. He had to pass through Samaria and therefore came to a city called Sychar, near the piece of land that Jacob gave to his son Joseph. Jacob's well was there.

Jesus was tired from the trip and sat by the well.[1] It was about the sixth hour, noon or a little later. A Samaritan woman came to draw water, and Jesus said to her, "May I have a drink?" His students were in town buying food.

The Samaritan woman said, "Why do you, a Jew, ask me for a drink? I'm a Samaritan woman, and Jews don't have anything to do with Samaritans."[2]

Jesus answered, "If you knew about God's gifts and who it is asking for a drink, you could have asked him and he'd give you the water of life."

She said, "Sir, you have no bucket to get the water and the well is deep, so where do you get the water of life? You're not greater than our father Jacob, are you? He gave us this well, and he and his sons and his cattle drank from it."

Jesus said, "Anyone who drinks this water will get thirsty again. But the water I give will be a source of water for unending life."

The woman said, "Sir, give me some of this water so I won't get thirsty and have to come all this way to use the well."

He said, "Go get your husband and come here."

The woman said, "I don't have a husband."

3 Now the story takes a dark turn. Jesus reminds the woman that she has had five husbands, which, as many scholars have commented, may not be a moral complaint but simply an observation. It could be a psychological remark. Maybe she has had a complicated and difficult life and could not sustain a good relationship. Like a good therapist, Jesus is getting to the source of her discontent and the reason why she needs to reconnect with the source of her life. This is his method in general, getting to the heart of the matter and offering a deep remedy for profound suffering.

4 The story contains several reversals or ironies. Jesus asks for a drink, but he is the one who offers the living water. The woman tells Jesus that she knows a messiah is coming, and Jesus informs her that he is that very person. People may think of Jesus as a lone celibate surrounded by men and yet, as in this story, he often interacts meaningfully with women.

5 "Individuals with a messianic complex do exist today. It is usually necessary to institutionalize them. Such a person lives in an inner world which puts him out of communication with the world about him.... The likelihood is that [Jesus] did not identify himself with it."
—John R. Yungblut, *Rediscovering the Christ* (Rockport, MA: Element, 1974), 50

6 The fact that Jesus's followers are surprised to see him speaking with a woman indicates that they do not yet fully realize the revolution he brings. The old rules about gender inferiority belong to a dead culture. Jesus represents a new testament.

7 The woman leaves her water jar behind, and yet at the beginning it was the most important object in her life. Something has happened. Maybe the abandoned jar indicates that she no longer thinks practically and literally but metaphorically. The literal water is not going to solve the kind of thirst she has.

8 We did not hear about Jesus recounting the woman's whole life, but only the part about having five husbands. Maybe that fact sums up her life, or maybe Jesus did explore with her the rest of her life as an aspect of his therapeutic teaching. Going over a lifetime with a fresh imagination can be an important aspect of healing.

Jesus said, "Yes, you're right. You don't have a husband. You've had five husbands, and the one you have now is not really your husband. What you said is true."[3]

The woman said, "Sir, I gather you're a prophet. Our fathers worshipped on this mountain, but you people say that Jerusalem is where people should worship."

Jesus said, "Woman, trust me, the time is coming when you will worship the Father neither on this mountain nor in Jerusalem. You worship something you can't see. We worship what we can see. Jews have the key to being saved.

"The time is coming, and is here, in fact, when people will worship the Father in spirit and openness."

The woman said, "I know that a messiah is coming, called Christos. When he comes he will explain all this to us."[4]

Jesus said, "Yes, and this man is talking with you now. I am he."[5]

At this point the followers returned and were surprised to see him speaking with a woman, though no one asked, "What do you want?" or "Why are you talking to her?"[6]

The woman left her water jar behind[7] and went to town and told people there, "Come and see a man who told me all the things I've done in my life. Could he be Christos?"[8]

Those people left town and came to see Jesus.

9 Throughout this passage about the Samaritan woman we hear Jesus talking at another, generally metaphorical or spiritual, level. He seems almost out of touch with conventional language and ordinary reality. This is an example of how he always teaches poetically and in metaphor.

10 "Eternal life requires the transformation of the inner Human."
   —Karen L. King, *The Gospel of Mary of Magdala: Jesus and the First Woman Apostle* (Santa Rosa, CA: Polebridge Press, 2003), 133

The eternal part of us is certainly involved in ordinary life, but it is not ruled by time and practicality.

11 When we follow the gospel teachings we are joining a tradition, whether or not we are part of a church or formal religion. Just as Jesus, his students, and John the Baptist have created this vision that could save us all from self-destruction, we can add to that work in our time and place. The calling is not just for personal gain but to help others.

12 Jesus saves us from what? From our self-serving tendencies that lead us to self-destruction, from our failure to achieve human community in which we can find safety and fulfillment.

13 This paragraph and the one before it point out that we recognize who and what Jesus is by hearing and seeing, through word and action. Both are essential. It makes no sense to be compassionate unless you act on the inner attitude and emotion.

Meanwhile the followers were urging him to eat. But he said, "I have food that you don't know about."[9]

The followers said to each other, "Did anyone bring him something to eat?"

Jesus said, "My food is to fulfill the desire of the one who sent me and to finish his work. Isn't there a saying, 'In four months the harvest will be here'? I'm telling you, open your eyes and look at the fields. They're no longer green. They're ready for the harvest.

"Even now the reaper is being paid and piling up rewards for eternal life.[10] Those who plant and those who harvest can be happy at the same time. In this regard, the saying is apropos: 'One person plants and another harvests.'

"I sent you to harvest crops that you have not worked on. Others have done the work and now you join in their labor."[11]

Many Samaritans in that town trusted in him because of what the woman told them, especially, "He told me all the things I've done in my life."

Therefore when the Samaritans went to see Jesus, they asked him to stay with them. He remained there for two days. Many more of them put their faith in him because of things he said. They told the woman, "We trust him now not because of what you told us but because of what we have heard for ourselves. We know that he is truly the savior of the world."[12]

After two days, he left and went to Galilee. Jesus often said that a prophet gets no honor in his own territory, but when he arrived in Galilee the people there welcomed him. They had seen the things he did at the festival in Jerusalem—they had been there.[13]

14 There are two aspects to Jesus's healing. One is the startling control over
   nature, the dazzle of instant healing. In its best light this aspect reveals that
   Jesus has a connection with a higher world. The other aspect is Jesus's compassion for human frailties and personal suffering.

He was in Cana of Galilee once again, where he had changed water into wine. A royal official there had a son who was ill in Capernaum. When he heard that Jesus had left Judea for Galilee, he went to him and begged him to come and heal his son. He was about to die. Jesus said, "Unless people see signs and wonders, they have little trust."[14]

The official said, "Please, sir. Come, before my child dies."

Jesus told him, "Go on. Your son is alive."

The man trusted Jesus's word and went off. As he was hurrying down, his servants met him and told him that his son was alive. He asked them exactly when the child started getting better. They said, "Yesterday, the fever left at the seventh hour."

The father knew that it was precisely at that moment when Jesus told him, "Your son is alive." He and his entire household put their trust in Jesus. And this was a second sign that Jesus did after he returned to Galilee from Judea.

1   This is the third striking story in the Book of John, and the third to offer an image of living water. The first was the water in jars at the wedding party, the second in Jacob's well with the Samaritan woman, and now a pool. Three kinds of containers and sources: jar, well, and pool. In each case the water becomes alive, first through Jesus's words, then through Jesus's mythmaking, and now through the work of an angel. Often the water that heals indicates it is alive; in this case it is stirred by the angel.

2   At the wedding party in Cana, Jesus did not actually perform a miracle. He simply told the waiters to taste the water now, and it was wine. Here again Jesus does not perform a miracle. You might expect him to find a way to get the man into the pool and be healed there. Otherwise, why all the details about the angel and moving water? He simply tells the sick man to pick up his mat and discover that he has been healed. In these instances, Jesus does not exactly heal but shows us that we are healthy, whereas before we thought we were sick.

3   Incredibly, people often think, even today, that it is more important to keep some arbitrary religious rule than to be healed of a thirty-eight-year-old illness.

4   Some would interpret this statement in terms of Jesus's divine sonship, but you could also understand it as the divine or infinite capacity in us all. We, too, can break ritual rules for a higher purpose.

Chapter 5

After this there was a Jewish festival, so Jesus went to Jerusalem. In the city there is a pool[1] by the sheep gate that in Hebrew is called Bethesda. It has five porticoes. In these shelters many sick, disabled, blind, and withered people wait for the waters to move. An angel comes down at various times and stirs the waters. Once the water moves, whoever is first to step in is cured of whatever illness he's suffering from.

One man who was there had been sick for thirty-eight years. Jesus saw him lying down and could tell that he had been there a long time. "Do you want to get well?" he asked.

The sick man said, "Sir, I have no one to put me in the pool when the water moves. When I start to move down, someone always steps in ahead of me." Jesus said, "Get up, pick up your mat, and walk."[2]

Instantly the man got better, picked up his mat, and walked.

It happened to be the Sabbath, and some Jews said to the man who had gotten better, "It's the Sabbath. You're not allowed to pick up your mat and walk. Who told you to do this?"[3]

The man didn't know who helped him, for Jesus had slipped away while a crowd filled the place. Later, Jesus came across him in the temple and said, "Look, you're looking better. Don't misbehave anymore. You don't want something worse to happen."

The man went away and told the Jews that it was Jesus who had helped him. This is why the Jews picked on Jesus, because he was doing things like this on the Sabbath.

He told them, "My Father is at work now, and so am I."[4]

Jesus was not only dishonoring the Sabbath, he was also referring to God as his own father, making himself God's equal. So the Jews conspired to kill him.

5 "For the man of traditional societies there exists a perfect *porosity* between all cosmic planes."
> —Mircea Eliade, *Journal I, 1945–1955*, trans. Mac Linscott Ricketts (Chicago: University of Chicago Press, 1990), 24

6 Jesus's power derives from his attunement with the highest realms, with the sky or the heavens, and the infinite. They are the domain of his "Father." But we can all enjoy a similar attunement and live by higher values and even have the power offered by such a sublime attitude.

7 This is the teaching, expressed in various ways, of many spiritual traditions. I am not attached to my will or ego but to the will of the one who put me in this life. The Zen master says, "Wherever you go you should be the master of your surroundings. This means you should not lose your way. This is called Buddha, because if you exist in this way always, you are Buddha himself. Without trying to be Buddha you are Buddha" (Suzuki).

"Thus the Master lives in perfect serenity, arms open to whatever life brings him, whereas the unaware person walks on the edge of danger, continually trying to keep one step ahead of fate."
> —Stephen Mitchell, *The Second Book of the Tao* (New York: Penguin, 2009), 60

Jesus said to them, "What I'm saying is that the son can't do anything himself unless he sees the Father doing it. Whatever the Father does, the son does in the same way.[5]

"The Father loves the son and reveals to him everything that he does. The Father will show him even more impressive things than this, so much greater that you'll be astonished. The Father raises the dead and gives them life, and the son, too, gives life to anyone he wants.[6] The Father doesn't evaluate people. He has given all that power of judgment to the son.

"Everyone will honor the son just as they now honor the Father. Whoever doesn't honor the son doesn't honor the Father who sent him. Listen closely: Whoever hears what I say and trusts in the one who sent me will enjoy eternity in life. He won't be evaluated. He'll have gone from death to life.

"The time is coming, and in fact is here now, when the lifeless will hear the son of God's voice and they will be alive. Just as the Father is his own source of life, so he allows the son to have his own source of life. He gave the son the authority to discern things, because he is a son of man, a human being.

"Don't be surprised at this. The time is coming when people in their graves will hear his voice. They'll come out. If they lived good lives, they'll come out to a resurrected life. If they were evil, to a resurrection of condemnation.

"I can do nothing on my own. I make decisions by what I hear. My decisions are good because I'm not attached to my own will but the wishes of the one who sent me.[7] If I talk about myself on my own terms, my descriptions are inaccurate. But if another talks about me, I know that what he says is right.

8   We often think of the Hebrew Bible writings as forerunners of Jesus or as preparing for him. Here he says more plainly that they are about him. They are about anyone who embodies the laws of life in his or her behavior and attitude. Our task is not just to learn from Jesus, the embodiment of the way of life—what the Chinese call "Tao" and Jesus "Father"—but to be him, insofar as he shows us how to do the Father's will.

9   "Before the time of my knowledge, I lay in great strife until I received my noble crown. Then I first learned to know how God does not dwell in the external fleshly heart, but in the soul's *centrum*, in itself."
      —Jacob Boehme, *The Way to Christ*, trans. Peter Erb (New York: Paulist Press, 1978), 264

10 People are drawn to those who are successful on the world stage but not to those who pristinely live in tune with the laws and values of life. We like egos but have trouble with those who obey a deeper law.

"You consulted John, and what he says is right. But what I say doesn't come from a man. I say these things so that you can be safe. He was a lamp burning and shining, and you were happy for a time in his light. But what I have to say is more important than what John said. The Father has given me a job to do, and this job is to let you know that the Father sent me.

"The Father who sent me has spoken for me. You have never heard his voice or seen his shape. You don't have his words in you because you don't trust the one he sent. You scour the scriptures because you think that you'll find timeless life in them. But these writings are about me.[8] Are you willing to be with me and have eternity in life?[9]

"I don't receive praise from people. But I do know that you don't have the love of God in you. I've come in my Father's name, and you don't welcome me. If someone else appears in his own name, you'll welcome him.[10]

"How can you trust when you receive honors from one another but not from the one and only God? Do you think that I will accuse you before the Father? No, the accuser is Moses, even though you place all your hope in him.

"If you believe Moses, you should believe in me. He wrote about me. But if you don't trust what he said, how can you place your trust in my words?"

1 This story contains one of Jesus's main points: His teaching is a leaven, like a small quantity of yeast in a large bowl of flour. Though small, it makes all the difference and has gigantic effect. This is certainly true today. If people loved each other consistently and in spite of differences, the world would be entirely different. Metanoia—*meta*, as in metamorphosis, a radical change, like the one from worm to butterfly, and *noia*, knowledge or the order of the world—is a slight shift in attitude and way of thinking, but it could transform human culture. The teaching is like a few loaves of bread and two fish for feeding a huge crowd.

2 There is always symbolism in the numbers used in the Gospel stories. Twelve baskets echo the twelve apostles, which echo the twelve tribes of Israel. But more importantly, the bread and fish represent Jesus's role in nourishing the soul with his teaching and example. Bible scholar John Dominic Crossan says that this story reflects a ritual among early Christians that features a meal of bread and fish, representing the life of Jesus and his use of commensality, bringing all sorts of people to the table (Crossan).

3 Notice that they do not call him a wonder-worker but a prophet. Unconsciously we think of "miracles" as proof of Jesus's otherworldly nature. But perhaps the people are impressed by his ability to express profound spiritual truths, as did the prophets of old.

Chapter 6

After this Jesus went to the other side of the Sea of Galilee. A big crowd was with him, watching the things he was doing for the sick. And then he went up on a mountain and sat down with his followers. The Jewish Passover was approaching. Jesus looked up and saw that a large crowd was coming together and said to Philip, "Where are we going to buy bread so that everyone can eat?"

He said this to tease him because he knew what he was going to do. But Philip said, "Two hundred denarii worth of bread isn't enough for everyone to have even a little."

One of the followers, Andrew, Simon Peter's brother, said, "There's a young man here with five loaves of barley bread and two fish, but what use are these for so many people?"[1]

Jesus said, "Tell the people to sit down." There was a wide expanse of grass there, so the people sat, about five thousand of them. Then Jesus took the loaves of bread, gave thanks, and shared them with everyone. He did the same with the fish, as much as they wanted. When they were full, he told his followers, "Gather up the leftovers so that nothing is wasted." They gathered them up and filled twelve baskets[2] with the pieces of the barley bread. When the people saw the wonder he had performed, they said, "This is really a prophet who has come into the world."[3] Jesus saw that they were thinking of taking hold of him forcefully and making him king, so he withdrew to the mountain by himself.

4   John Dominic Crossan says that the word *epi*, usually translated *"on* the water" could be "near" or "by" the water. "The point is not to diminish the miracle but to keep the focus where it should be, not on the general power of Jesus but on the specific impotence of the disciples without him" (Crossan). Given the choice of words, I use *by* to help us rethink the scene. The deep spiritual teaching of Jesus can be lost in the bright glow of miracles. On the other hand, walking on water gets your attention and has become an instant image for a different relationship to nature. That, too, is rich and beneficial.

5   The issue seems to be Jesus finding his own way. Story after story portrays him with his students or with crowds where he teaches and heals—occasionally alone praying—so to imagine him going off on his own may seem strange. But it may be good to think of him having his own life now and then.

6   This is yet another opportunity to reflect on metaphor as a way to get to the heart of the matter. Jesus says it is important to concentrate more on nourishment of the soul than just the body, and you get your attention in the right place by not taking this literally. This is a key point for anyone seeking genuine spiritual guidance from the Gospels. And once again, Jesus sounds like an alchemist whose entire purpose was to appreciate physical material as metaphor for the realm of spirit.

7   Exodus 16:4; Psalm 78:24.

When evening came, his followers went to the lake. They got into a boat and started crossing to Capernaum. It was dark and Jesus hadn't joined them yet. A strong wind came up and stirred up the lake. They had gone out about four miles when they saw Jesus walking by the water, approaching their boat.[4] They were surprised.

He said, "Don't worry. It's me."

They wanted to take him in their boat, and in no time they were at the shore they were heading for. The next day a crowd stood on the other side of the lake and noticed that there were no small boats there, except one. So Jesus had not gone with his followers in a boat. The followers must have gone alone.

A number of small craft from Tiberias came near the place where the people had eaten the bread and Jesus had given thanks. So when the crowd saw that Jesus and his circle weren't there, they got into the small boats and went to Capernaum looking for him. When they found him on the other side of the lake, they said, "Rabbi, when did you get here?"[5]

Jesus said, "You want me because you ate the bread and felt full, not because you witnessed wonders. Don't do anything for food that perishes but for the kind that endures and is timeless.[6] The son of man will give this kind of food to you. The Father has given him his approval."

They said, "Then what should we do to be involved in the work of God?"

He said, "To trust in the one he sent is the work of God."

They said, "Then what kind of sign will you do for us so that we can see what is happening and can trust you? What will you do? Our fathers ate manna in the wilderness. It's written, 'He gave them bread from the sky to eat.'"[7]

8 "The 'earth' or 'world' can be our individual and more or less sensorial soul as well as the ambience in which we live and which determines us, just as 'Heaven' can be our spiritual virtualities as well as the paradisal worlds; for 'the kingdom of God is within you.'"

> —Frithjof Schuon, *The Fullness of God*, ed. James S. Cutsinger (Bloomington, IN: World Wisdom, 2004), 34

The word *sky* here stands for the inner spiritual or soul layer of existence. We need ordinary bread to stay alive physically, but we also need the food of Jesus's vision, which is from the sky and not the literal earth, for our souls.

9 Jesus can be our teacher and guide not for any miracles he can perform but because he is the rare human being open to the influence of the sky and the paternal guidance found by turning attention away from the literal. He promises to be ever close to the Father's guidance and always present for other human beings in order to give them what he has received. You hear this point again and again in the Book of John. Jesus is the intermediary, similar to a shaman whose ways of being inspired and guided are extraordinary in the extreme.

10 The following are the opening words of the "Prologue" to Nikos Kazantzakis's *The Last Temptation of Christ*: "The dual substance of Christ—the yearning, so human, so superhuman, of [humanity] to attain to God, or, more exactly, to return to God and identify himself with him—has always been a deep inscrutable mystery to me. This nostalgia for God, at once so mysterious and so real, has opened in me large wounds and also large flowing springs" (Kazantzakis).

"But Moses didn't give you bread from the sky," he said. "My Father gives you the real bread that comes from the sky. God's bread comes from the sky and gives life to the world."[8]

They said, "Sir, give us this kind of bread always."

Jesus said, "I am the bread of life. Whoever comes to me will never be hungry and whoever trusts in me will never be thirsty. But as I said, you have seen me and yet don't trust me. Whatever the Father gives me I will hold tight, and whoever comes to me I will never push away.[9]

"I have come from above not for my own purposes but for the one who sent me. He doesn't want me to lose anyone he's given me but rather to resurrect him on the last day. My Father's intent is that anyone who really sees the son and trusts in him will have eternity in life, and I will resurrect him on the last day."[10]

The Jews were murmuring about Jesus because he had said, "I am the bread that came from above." They said, "This is Jesus, son of Joseph. We know his mother and father. How can he say, 'I have come from above'?"

11 What does it mean to be resurrected? Is this an after-death experience, or is it a completely new life in this world after having been dull, unconscious, and self-destructive? The new rules of the game that Jesus offers promises a new life, an awakening, and, in a deeply personal way, a resurrection.

12 Isaiah 54:13

13 If you have trust in the way of life Jesus embodies and teaches, you will not be time bound or caught in the trap of materialism. You will have access to the infinite possibilities represented by the sky. Your life will have a timeless quality. You will appreciate the mythic and archetypal dimensions of your experience. You will be connected to the most profound mysteries and sense the endless depth of your existence. This discovery is liberating. Jesus says over and over that being exposed to him is your route to the infinite. I translate the Greek words *zoen aionon*—"life of the eons"—as "eternity in life." The Greek word *aion* does not mean just time past but life before life, the origins of life, who we are before we are. To trust that these teachings represent the way of the eternal puts you in touch with your most profound origins.

14 The key in this teaching is to understand "life" as more than survival. It refers to being vital emotionally, intellectually, and spiritually. Obviously, when Jesus says "eat me," he is not speaking literally. You ingest his teachings and assimilate them, merging them with your life. You are fed by them. At the same time, this eating could refer to the ritual of the Eucharist, eating Jesus in the special rite of Communion.

15 Again, this does not mean that if you eat this heavenly bread you will never die physically. In tune with the other statements in this section, it can mean that you will live on a different plane and in a different kind of time. *Aion*, the key Greek word used in this section, refers to the time of an eternal condition. Maybe the words of the renowned philosopher of religion Mircea Eliade can clarify. He frequently uses the Latin phrase *in illo tempore*, meaning in that time, not this one, the time of myth, of events that took place outside of history and serve as powerful guides for our lives today. "Living a myth implies a genuine religious experience, since it differs from the ordinary experience of everyday life ... not a commemoration of mythical events but a reiteration of them.... One becomes their contemporary.... One is no longer living in chronological time but in the primordial time" (Eliade).

Jesus responded. "Don't murmur among yourselves. No one can come to me unless the Father who sent me draws him near, and then I'll resurrect him on the last day.[11] The prophets wrote, 'And they will all be instructed about God.'[12] Anyone who has heard and learned from the Father comes to me. No one has seen the Father except the one who is from God. He has seen the Father, and whoever has deep trust has eternity in life.[13]

"I'm the bread of life. Your fathers ate manna in the wilderness and then died. My bread comes from the sky. Anyone who eats it doesn't die. I am the living bread that came from the sky, and anyone who eats this bread will live forever. The bread that I will give for the sake of the world's life is my flesh."

The Jews argued about this, too. "How can this man give us his flesh to eat?"

Jesus said, "Unless you eat the flesh of the son of man and drink his blood, you'll be without life. Whoever eats my flesh and drinks my blood will have eternity in life. I'll resurrect him on the last day. My flesh is real food and my blood real drink. Whoever eats my flesh and drinks my blood abides in me and I in him. Just as the living Father sent me and I live because of the Father, so anyone who eats me will be alive through me.[14]

"This bread came from the sky. It's not like the bread of the fathers. They ate it and then died. Anyone who eats this bread will be alive forever."[15]

16 This is not to deny the value of a sensuous bodily existence but to point out that the physical world is incomplete without the eternal. Time without eternity is meaningless and unbearable. In fact, we are not fully human if we do not include the spiritual and timeless. Today it is common to reduce human experience to biology, genetics, and brain studies. But this is exactly the kind of limited thinking that Jesus speaks against. His words are filled with spirit and vitality.

17 Once again we find a reference to *zoen aionon*, life outside of time.

18 C. G. Jung invites us to see the presence of Judas as one among the Twelve as a universal, mythic situation in which the good hero is thwarted by someone in his own company. Jung says that any of us might be Judas at some time in our lives, either through conscious intention or by the force of circumstances. We betray those we admire and even love, and by so doing usually complete the hero's initiation (Jung).

The American psychologist James Hillman also analyzes the Judas figure as a necessity, and he cites the story of Jesus as an example: "Betrayal is essential to the dynamics of the climax of the Jesus story and thus betrayal is at the heart of the Christian mystery.... The message of love, the Eros mission of Jesus, carries its final force only through the betrayal and crucifixion. For at the moment when God lets him down, Jesus becomes truly human, suffering the human tragedy" (Hillman).

He said all these things in the synagogue where he taught in Capernaum. Some of his followers on hearing all this said, "What you say is very challenging. Who can handle it?"

Jesus, knowing that his followers were complaining, said, "Does what I say shock you? What happens if you see the son of man going back up where he was previously? The spirit gives life. The flesh doesn't give you anything.[16] My words are spirit and life.

"But some of you can't put your trust in it." Jesus knew at first that there were some who didn't trust in him. He knew who would betray him.

He said, "This is why I keep saying no one can come to me unless the Father allows it."

As a result many of his followers withdrew and didn't stay with him. Jesus said to the Twelve, "You don't want to go away, too, do you?"

Simon Peter replied, "Sir, to whom shall we go? You have words of eternal life.[17] We have believed in you and know that you are the holy one of God."

Jesus said, "I chose the Twelve of you myself, but one of you is a devil."

He was referring to Judas, the son of Simon Iscariot. He was one of the Twelve and was about to betray him.[18]

1 This is quite a sentence about a figure such as Jesus, whose mission in life is to save the world from its own ignorance and compulsions. He has to go, apparently furtively, from place to place to avoid assassins. John's Gospel has a thriller aspect as well as a spiritual teaching one.

2 Next we have a typical family interaction, as Jesus's brothers—or close companions, if you prefer—goad him into being more public. "Don't be so secretive," they seem to be saying, their advice contradicting Jesus's movements aimed at avoiding assassination.

3 More thriller material.

4 This is one of the great mysteries of life: how human beings often divide themselves into two opposite opinions with little or no middle ground. Some people admired Jesus and others despised him. So it is today. Present a new idea, even one full of compassion and humanitarianism, and some will be grateful and others critical.

5 Many things in life must be learned, but Jesus did not get his extraordinary insight into human suffering, wrongdoing, and illness from school. He goes on to say that he is in tune with the universe. He knows things intuitively.

Chapter 7

Jesus moved around from place to place in Galilee. He didn't want to go about in Judea because the Jews were looking for a way to assassinate him.[1] The Jewish festival of Tabernacles was approaching, and his brothers told him, "Let's get out of here and go to Judea so your followers there can see the wonderful things you're doing. If a person wants the public to notice him, he doesn't work in secret. If you're doing this powerful work, let the world see you."[2]

Even his brothers were having trouble believing in him.

Jesus replied, "The time isn't right for me. For you it's always a good time. The world can't hate you, but it rejects me because I speak out. When I see people acting wickedly, I say something. Why don't you go to the festival yourselves. I won't go because my time isn't here yet."

He said all this and then stayed in Galilee. But when his brothers had left for the festival, he went to it, too, secretly.

At the festival the Jews looked for him, wondering where he might be.[3] Various other groups were arguing about him. Some said, "He's a good man." Others said, "No, he's leading people astray."[4] None of them said anything in public for fear of the Jews.

In the midst of the festival Jesus went into the temple and taught. The Jews were amazed. "How did this man become so learned without an education?"[5]

6   Here is a key psychological insight into spiritual leadership. You are a con-
    duit. You let a profound inspiration stream through you and use your voice.
    No ego. No fame.

7   The word *daimon* often appears in the original Greek version of the Gospels,
    and it is usually translated "demon." But daimon, both in the ancient world
    and in modern depth psychology, has a different meaning. It is the inner
    voice or sense of direction, sometimes the voice of conscience, that directs
    us usually from within. You might rarely actually hear a voice that seems to
    guide you. Socrates said that his daimon was a love spirit, and the existential
    psychiatrist Rollo May described it as an important inner guide. I use the
    word *daimon* because it does not necessarily imply anything negative.

8   Sometimes it is not easy to distinguish some forms of insanity from inspira-
    tion. Or maybe people intuitively recognize the voice of inspiration speak-
    ing through a person. In any case, the crowd is not far off from understanding
    how Jesus, as he keeps saying, speaks for the Father.

9   As before, the people seem confused about how any ordinary person can
    be in their midst as one of them and at the same time be inspired. How can
    Jesus be so eloquent and yet come from a family everyone knows? This is
    a crucial point about the spiritual life, how the spiritual can manifest in the
    ordinary.

10 This section offers a fascinating exploration of what some call the divinity
    within the human. As many mystics attest, they do not choose to speak
    divinely but somehow have been selected for the job. Jesus is indeed close
    to the Father who sent him, so close that the only way to know the Father is
    through Jesus.

Jesus responded to this question. "My teaching isn't my own. It comes from the one who sent me. If you want to try out his plan, you should be able to discern whether these ideas come from God or whether I'm just speaking for myself. Whoever talks from his own resources is usually looking for fame. But if he's really seeking honor for the one who sent him, then he's genuine. He has no personal agenda.[6]

"Moses gave you the law, and yet none of you actually lives out the law. Why do you want to kill me?"

The people replied, "Your daimon is talking.[7] Are you crazy?[8] Who wants to kill you?"

Jesus said, "I did one remarkable thing, and you're all shocked. Moses gave you the practice of circumcision. It didn't come originally from Moses but from his ancestors. You circumcise a man on the Sabbath. Now, if you circumcise a man on the Sabbath and the law of Moses isn't broken, why are you upset with me because I made a man perfectly well on the Sabbath? Don't judge me superficially. Be serious and thoughtful."

Some in Jerusalem were saying, "Isn't this the man they want to assassinate? Look, he's speaking in public and they're saying nothing to him. Don't these leaders think he's Christos, the Man of Oil? On the other hand, we know where this man is from. When Christos appears, no one will know his origins."[9]

Then Jesus spoke up. "You know me and you know where I come from. I don't come here by my own choosing.[10] I was sent here by someone you don't know but who is real. I know him because I am close to him and he sent me."

They were looking for a way to apprehend him, but no one laid a hand on him since it wasn't his time. Many in the crowd believed in him. "When Christos comes, he couldn't perform more signs than this man has, could he?" they said.

11 The ordinary person cannot achieve the state of union Jesus describes with the Sky Father, who is both related to and far removed from ordinary life. It is as if an ordinary person said he or she wanted to join a shaman in his or her spirit travels. It cannot usually be done.

12 Throughout the Gospels we have seen hints of Greek spirituality peeking through in soft allusions to the gods and goddesses, such as the Dionysian implications of Jesus turning water into wine at Cana or saying that his blood is wine at the Last Supper. Here that connection is explicit in a rare reference to Jesus perhaps teaching the Greeks living in his area. If nothing else, it is a strong reminder of the close presence of Greek culture in Jesus's world.

13 One strong parallel in the Hebrew Bible is the scene in Exodus 17:6 where the people on their journey need water and beg Moses to do something about it. On the command of God, Moses strikes a rock with a power stick and water comes flowing out.

The image of water flowing from the center of the body is interesting as a yoga reference, the notion that there is a body center, here close to the abdomen, where spiritual, living water or fluid comes out.

The Pharisees noticed the people murmuring these things about Jesus, and the chief priests and the Pharisees sent officers to arrest him.

Jesus said, "I'll be with you for a short while, and then I'll go to the one who sent me. You'll look for me, but you won't find me. Where I am, you can't come."[11]

The Jews discussed this. "Where does this man plan on going where we can't find him? Could he be thinking of going to the diaspora among the Greeks to teach them?[12] What did he mean when he said, 'You'll look for me and not find me. Where I am you can't come'?"

On the last day of the festival, the day of the big dinner, Jesus stood up and spoke out, "If anyone is thirsty, he should come to me and drink. If a person trusts in me, as the scriptures say, rivers of living water will flow from the center of his body."[13]

He was talking about the spirit. People who believed in him would receive it, but not yet, since he had not yet come into his glory.

Some who heard what he had to say said, "There's no doubt that this is the prophet." Others said, "He is Christos." But still others wondered, "We can be sure that Christos is not going to come from Galilee. Doesn't the scripture say that Christos will be descended from David and come from Bethlehem, David's town?"

The people were divided in their opinion of him. Some wanted to arrest him, but still no one laid a hand on him. The officers returned to the chief priests and the Pharisees, and they said, "Why didn't you bring him in?"

The officers replied, "Never has a person spoken the way this man speaks."

14 In this passage you can sense how deeply the religious leaders have been stirred by the presence of Jesus. He seems to threaten the core of their belief. Nicodemus tries to be reasonable, but reason does not touch this kind of emotional turbulence. Psychologically, Jesus has opened a complex in them surrounding their rigid formulas and rules. It can happen to anyone overly caught up in the surfaces of his or her spiritual attachment. We can only imagine how this environment created a sense of danger for Jesus and his followers.

The Pharisees said, "You haven't been duped, too, have you? Not one of the leaders or the Pharisees believes in him. The people are stupid. They don't know the law. Let them be damned!"

Nicodemus, who was one of Jesus's followers and had visited him previously, said, "Our law doesn't judge a person until it first listens to him and knows exactly what he's up to."

The others said, "Are you from Galilee, too? Look it up. You'll see that no prophet is to come out of Galilee."[14]

At that point, everyone went home.

1   Some scholars think that this bit about tricking Jesus was not in the original
    story. If you leave it out, the Pharisees do not look malevolent They are
    simply asking for an opinion. For an extensive discussion of the role of the
    Pharisees in the Gospels, see Brad H. Young, "Save the Adultress! Ancient
    Jewish *Responsa* in the Gospels," *New Testament Studies* 41 (1995): 59–70.

    It is too easy to find an exaggerated foil for your hero, and perhaps that
    has been done too often at the expense of the Pharisees' reputation.

2   Scholars think that this story was not originally in this Gospel. Jesus's
    response to the Pharisees is a powerful one, because here he dramatically
    sidesteps the moralism that is often part of the spiritual life but has no
    place in Jesus's kingdom. Whatever the historical meaning of his writing
    in the sand, the gesture makes sense as an unexpected, dramatic, nonverbal
    response to a tense situation.

3   "It was worthwhile living to have said that."
        —Oscar Wilde, "De Profundis," in *De Profundis and Other Writings* (New York:
        Penguin, 1982), 177

Chapter 8

Jesus went off to the Mount of Olives and returned to the temple in the morning. The people came in great numbers and he sat and taught them.

The experts in the law and the Pharisees brought forward a woman caught in adultery. They put her in the center of the courtyard and said, "Teacher, this woman was caught in the act of adultery. In the law, Moses instructs us to stone a woman like this. What do you think?"[1]

They were trying to trick him so they could have reason to charge him.

Jesus bent over and made marks on the ground with his finger.[2] When they kept probing, he stood up and said, "Anyone here who has never made a serious mistake be the first one to throw a stone at her."[3]

Once again he stooped down and wrote on the ground.

When they heard what he said, they began to leave, one by one, beginning with the older ones. Jesus was left alone with the woman where she was standing in the center of the courtyard. He stood up and said, "Woman, where did they go? Didn't anyone condemn you?"

She said, "No one, sir."

Jesus said, "I don't condemn you either. Go now, and don't make the same mistakes."

4   The world is so full of intellectual cloudiness and unconscious behavior that
    we badly need light. We need to understand better what it is all about and
    how to relieve ourselves of the anxiety caused by dark ignorance and confu-
    sion. And so Jesus, with his remarkably clear and simple philosophy, under-
    girded by a sophisticated psychology, is the bearer of light.

5   This is a clever argument. It is like saying, legally you need two people to
    make an accusation, you and a witness. Well, my two are myself and the
    source of my insights.

6   To understand passages such as this, it might help to have a less literal image
    of the Father in your mind. Think of the Father as the mysterious source of
    life, in the world and in yourself, or as the guiding law of nature. To look
    deeply into Jesus's actions and his words is to glimpse this archetypal father-
    ing principle of life.

7   Again we have a clear statement about two different experiences of life:
    One is literal, materialistic, unconscious, and narcissistic, while the other
    is poetic, spiritual, aware, and compassionate. It is as though there are two
    worlds and communication between them is difficult, if not impossible.
    Many people live their entire lives thinking that life is all about physical
    survival and material pleasures. There is no "above" in their lives.

Jesus resumed speaking. "I am the light of the cosmos. Whoever follows me will not walk in darkness but will enjoy life's luminosity."[4]

The Pharisees told him, "You're talking from yourself. Your words aren't authentic."

Jesus answered, "If I speak for myself, my words are genuine because I know where I'm from and where I'm going. You don't know where I come from and where I'm headed. You see things only in terms of physical existence. I'm not criticizing anyone, but even when I do criticize, my criticisms are genuine. I'm not alone in them. The Father sent me and so he and I are both involved.

"Your own law says that the testimony of two people is valid. Well, I account for myself, and the Father who sent me accounts for me."[5]

They said, "Where is your Father?"

"You don't know me and you don't know my Father. If you knew me, you would know my Father, too."[6]

Jesus spoke these words in the treasury as he was teaching in the temple. No one arrested him because his moment, his *kairos*, had not yet arrived.

He spoke again. "I'll go away and you'll look for me. You'll die with your uncertainty, because where I'm going you can't come."

The Jews said, "Do you think he'll kill himself? He said, 'Where I'm going you can't come.'"

He said, "You're from below and I'm from above. You're of this world and I'm not of this world. That's why I said that you'll die in your uncertainty."[7]

They said, "Who are you?"

Jesus said, "What have I been saying all along? I have a lot to say to you and much to criticize. He who sent me is real, and I'm telling the world just what I've heard from him."

8 Ralph Waldo Emerson consistently advocated individual inspiration, as he says interestingly in his journals: "It seemed to me an impiety to be listening to one & another, when the pure Heaven was pouring itself into each of us, on the simple condition of obedience. To listen to any secondhand gospel is perdition of the First Gospel. Jesus was Jesus because he refused to listen to another, & listened at home" (Emerson).

9 Jesus is speaking in personifying language, and that style of expression may persuade some to think too literally. Consider a slightly less personifying way of putting this insight: The universe is in accord with the person who understands its nature, is not a materialist, and lives according to its best ways.

10 One of the most important things a person can do is discover how life works and how best to be in accord with the laws of life. But it is very difficult to arrive at that knowledge, or *gnosis*. Many teachings and teachers seem to have it right, but usually there is some twist in the teaching or in its presentation and reception that keeps a person away from genuine knowledge. If you can find your way to the right sources and a good understanding of them, this knowledge will liberate you.

11 The people's response here indicates that they cannot appreciate what Jesus is saying. They think that because they are related by birth to a system that promises knowledge, they can be certain of their understanding. But one of Jesus's central ideas is that being born into a religion does not automatically liberate you from ignorance and confusion. It does not always heal your blindness.

12 In a broader sense, it might seem that being religious would make you open to a deep spiritual understanding that would guide you and free you. But it does not work that way. You cannot understand the subtlety and depth of what Jesus is saying, because your beliefs prevent you from being open to it.

13 In these few words Jesus is offering a homespun example of how to learn from the archetypal Father, the deep fathering principle of life. Remember what it was like to be a child, and nearness to your parent alone gave you lessons in life.

They failed to understand that he was talking about the Father. So Jesus said, "When you lift up the son of man, then you'll know that I am he. I do nothing on my own. I say only what the Father instructs me to say.[8] The one who sent me is with me. He hasn't left me alone because I always do what pleases him."[9]

When he said these things, many people believed in him. To the Jews he said, "If you take my words to heart then you really are my followers. You will know what is accurate, and it will free you."[10]

They said, "We are Abraham's descendants and have never been enslaved to anyone. Why do you say, 'You'll be free'?"[11]

Jesus said, "Anyone who acts out of ignorance and confusion is the slave of ignorance. The slave doesn't stay in a house forever, but the son does remain forever. If the son makes you free, you will truly be free. I know that you are Abraham's descendants. But you want to kill me because what I'm saying doesn't find any welcome in you.[12]

"I talk about things that I've seen while at my Father's side. Don't you do things you heard from your father?"[13]

They said, "Abraham is our father."

14 The people are keeping their minds closed through attachment to their traditional religion and its leader, Abraham. But Jesus reminds them that Abraham did not keep his mind closed. He was open to continuing inspiration.

15 Jesus introduces a counter or shadow father, the devil. We have to distinguish between what we take to be the law of life from what is truly from
above.

16 This is an ever-present question in the spiritual life. How can you be sure
that the way you have chosen is the right way, or intelligent or worthy of
your commitment? How do you know that the way you are following is
genuine? Jesus says here that the only way to find the right path is to be a
godly person or, translated more literally from the Greek, to be "from God."
     But this is not a good enough answer, because many people feel they are
godly when their belief actually gets in the way of being open to inspiration
from above. And so the discussion continues.

17 In other words, "Are you out of your mind?"

18 As usual, the people take Jesus literally. He is not talking about literal death
but the kind of death that keeps you from being fully alive during your
lifetime—the death principle. So here is another way of framing the question being discussed here: How can you live by the law of the Father, "from
above"?

Jesus said, "If you're Abraham's children, act like it. The way things are, you want to kill me, a person who has told you what is real and what I heard from God. Abraham didn't do this. You're not acting like your father."[14]

They said, "We weren't born out of wedlock. We have only one Father, God."

Jesus said, "If God were your Father, you would love me. I emerged from God and have come from him. I didn't decide to come; he sent me. Why don't you understand what I'm saying? Because you can't hear my message.

"You are children of the devil, and you want to do what that father wants.[15] From day one he was a murderer. He isn't genuine because he doesn't have any authenticity in him. When he lies, he's revealing his nature, for he's a liar, indeed the father of lies.

"Because what I say is genuine, you don't trust me. Which one of you could charge me with depravity? If I speak the truth, why don't you believe me? If someone is godly, he hears what God says. You don't hear it because you're not godly."[16]

The Jews replied, "Are we correct in saying that you're a Samaritan and are possessed by a daimon?"[17]

Jesus said, "I don't have a daimon. I give honor to my Father and you dishonor me. I'm not looking for glory. But there is one who observes and judges.

"Listen to what I'm saying. If anyone were to take my message to heart, he would never see death."

The Jews said, "Now we know that you have a daimon. Abraham died, and the prophets, too. But you say that if anyone takes your message to heart he won't taste death. Are you saying that you're greater than our father Abraham, who died? The prophets died, too. Who do you think you are?"[18]

19 Again we have a contrast between what the people mean by "God" and what Jesus means. Jesus speaks in a Gnostic or mystical style in which he can talk about he and the Father being one. If your idea of God is more literal, this identification is difficult to appreciate.

20 Jesus's teaching is contingent in some ways on his history and environment, but in other ways it is timeless. As the Logos, he was certainly present to Abraham, but as a human being he would not have been. Jesus and his accusers find it difficult to speak across these divides, as do people today who do not appreciate the mystical aspect of Jesus and his teaching. The great advantage of John's Gospel is to sustain the mystical aspect of Jesus and his words.

21 Scholars remind us that the "I am" statements of Jesus evoke the God of the Hebrew Bible. See Exodus 3:14 for an example. It is a way for Jesus to say differently that he and the Father are one. The people, taking him too literally, are outraged by these very statements. Today, the reader faces a similar problem, only many people today simply believe naively in an anthropomorphic God. In that case, they may find it difficult to read the Book of John and accept Jesus's statements that so closely connect him to the Father.

Jesus answered, "If I make myself shine, that's nothing. It's my Father who gives me glory. You say, 'He is our God,' yet you don't really know him. I know him.[19] If I said I didn't, I'd be a liar like you. I do know him and take his message to heart. Your father Abraham was happy when I appeared. He witnessed it and was glad."[20]

The Jews said, "You're not fifty yet and yet you've seen Abraham?"

Jesus said, "Before Abraham was born, I am."[21]

They picked up stones to throw at him, but he vanished from their sight and went out of the temple.

1   This chapter begins with yet another nuance in the development of a more
    mature spirituality. Religious people are often moralistic, too eager to blame
    others for not doing the right thing. Here, the people assume that the blind
    man must be suffering from someone's bad behavior.

2   In the Greek there is a slight play on words here. The question is, why is the
    man blind? The answer: So God's message can be seen.

    We have seen how Greek gods sometimes hide in the language of the
    Gospels. In this case, it is Phanes, the great god of Orphic religion, whose
    name means "bring to light." Notice the several references to night and day
    and light in general, all in the spirit of the Orphics.

3   In the darkness of humanity's failure to understand how the planet can thrive
    and humanity can live in global community, Jesus's embodiment of a deeper
    law is light. Jesus correctly predicts that night is coming on. Since the time
    of Jesus and his saving message, world history has darkened with the sav-
    agery of wars, the oppression of people everywhere, and the degradation of
    the natural world.

Chapter 9

While out walking, Jesus encountered a man who was blind from birth. His followers inquired, "Rabbi, who is at fault, this man here or his parents—why is he blind?"[1]

"Neither the man himself nor his parents are to blame," Jesus said. "This happened to him so that God's message might be visible through his experience.[2] While we have daylight, we have to do the work of the one who sent me. Night is coming on. Then we can't do this work. While I am in the world, I am the light of the world."[3]

After saying this, he spat on the ground and made mud with the saliva and packed it on the man's eyes. "Go and wash in the pool of Siloam." (The word means "sent.")

So the man went and washed and came out with his sight intact. His neighbors, knowing him previously as a beggar, said, "Isn't this the man who used to sit and beg?"

Some said, "Yes, he's the one." But others said, "No, it's someone like him." He himself said repeatedly, "It's me."

They asked him, "How were your eyes opened?"

4   The use of saliva and dirt for healing, especially for blindness, is well known in the ancient world. "Spittle, blood, sperm, sweat, nails and hair became magical substances ... because, after leaving the body, they would retain some essence of that person" (Eliade). Here, Jesus's essence mixes with earth to create a healing salve. If the reference to magic seems inappropriate, think of personal power.

"This man they call Jesus made clay and anointed my eyes and told me to go to Siloam and wash them. So I went and washed them out and began to see."[4]

"Where is he?" they asked.

"I don't know."

People brought this man to the Pharisees. It was on the Sabbath that Jesus made the clay and cleared his eyes. Again the Pharisees asked him how he regained his sight, and he told them, "This man put clay on my eyes, I washed them, and now I can see."

A few of the Pharisees said, "This man can't be from God. He doesn't respect the Sabbath."

But others said, "How could a depraved man perform these signs?"

They were divided about it all.

Once again they asked the blind man, "What do you think of him, since he cleared your eyes?"

He said, "The man's a prophet."

The Jews didn't believe that he had been blind and recovered his sight. They consulted his parents and asked them, "Is this one your son? You say that he was born blind? Then how do you explain the fact that he can see now?"

The parents answered, "Yes, we know that this is our son, and yes, he was born blind. Now he can see. How? We have no idea. Who cleared his eyes? We don't know. Ask him. He's old enough."

The parents spoke this way because they were afraid of the Jews. The Jews had already decided that if anyone said that Jesus was Christos, he was to be excluded from the synagogue. That's why his parents said, "He's old enough. Ask him."

A second time they called up the blind man and said, "Give glory to God. We know that this man Jesus is a wicked person."

The blind man said, "I don't know if he's wicked. All I know is that I was blind and now I see."

5 It seems to be a mark of human nature to be skeptical at all costs. Especially in the modern world, we hold back our assent until we have unassailable empirical proof. Here the extreme skepticism is comical. It also hides a deep need to keep old beliefs intact.

6 A touch of irony. The blind man has seen the son of man.

7 This is the familiar paradox in which those who think they know, do not; and those who should not know, do.

8 This interesting passage reminds us not to be only literal about the various "healings" but to also look more deeply into them. It also encourages us not to join those who are complacent about their philosophies. Those who think they see may be blind. Those who think they do not see may not be blind.

They asked him, "What did he do to you? How did he clear up your eyes?"

"How many times have I told you? You aren't listening. Why do you want to hear all this again? Do you want to be his followers, too?"

They got angry with him. "You may be his follower, but we're followers of Moses. We know that God spoke to Moses. We don't know where this man is from."

"What a thing," the man said. "You don't know where he's from. But he cleared up my eyes. We know full well that God doesn't listen to wicked people. But if someone is God-fearing and obedient, he does listen to him. In all of time never has anyone told of someone clearing up the eyes of a person who was born blind. If this man were not from God, he could do nothing."

They said, "You were born in the deepest ignorance and wickedness, and you're trying to teach us?" They sent him away.[5]

Jesus heard that they had sent the man away, so he found him and said, "Do you believe in the son of man?"

He said, "Who is he, sir, so I can believe in him?"

Jesus said, "Oh, you've seen him.[6] He's the one who is speaking with you now."

"Then I believe," the man said. And he offered Jesus a gesture of respect.

Jesus said, "I came into this world to sort things out, so that those who don't see, see, and those who see, become blind."[7]

The Pharisees that were with him heard this and said, "Are we also blind?"

Jesus said, "If you were blind, you wouldn't be so ignorant. But precisely because you say, 'We see,' your profound ignorance remains in place."[8]

1   Jesus begins his beloved and beautiful story of the good shepherd by hinting
    that you know whom to follow in the spiritual realm through recognition.
    You use your senses and intuition more than fear or mental powers. In this
    Jesus echoes Plato, who said that all real knowledge is a form of remember-
    ing. You know the most important things deep inside you but forget them.
    When you follow Jesus, you are recalling what you know already but recog-
    nize in Jesus's teaching.

2   What does it mean to have life abundantly? It could be more intensity, a
    greater range of experience, real intimacy, meaningful events, deep reflec-
    tion, felt beauty, friendship and community, and a strong connection with
    the natural world. If the major gifts of the spiritual life are vision and com-
    passion, the gift of life is from the soul.

Chapter 10

"Let me give you a practical metaphor. The person who enters a sheep pen, not by the gate but by climbing in some other way, is a thief and a cheat. The one who enters by the gate is the shepherd. The watchman opens the gate for him, and the sheep listen for his voice. He addresses his sheep by name and leads them out.[1]

"When he has led all his own sheep outside, they'll follow his lead because they know his voice. They would never follow a stranger—they'd run away from him because they wouldn't recognize his voice."

Jesus used this example, but they didn't get it. He tried once more.

"I'm the gate for the sheep. All those who came earlier were thieves and cheats. The sheep didn't listen to them. I'm the gate. If you enter through me, you'll be safe. You'll come and go and find a pasture. The thief comes to steal, kill, and destroy. I have come so that they will have life and have it more abundantly.[2]

"I am the good shepherd. The good shepherd lays down his life for his sheep. The hired hand is not the shepherd who owns the sheep. When he sees a wolf coming, he leaves the sheep and gets out of there. The wolf attacks the flock and routs them. The hired hand runs away. He doesn't care enough about the sheep.

"I'm the good shepherd. I know my sheep and my sheep know me. This is like the Father knowing me and me knowing the Father. I lay down my life for the sheep. I have other sheep, too, that are not part of this flock. I bring them, too. They listen to my voice. There will be one flock and one shepherd. My Father loves me because I give up my life and take it up again.

3   A strong theme in the Book of John is Jesus's embrace of his fate and his
    hope in resurrection. This approach makes all the difference in the lives of
    us all. We do not blame any misfortune on others but understand it as a con-
    sequence of our intensity of life. We also hope in some form of resurrection.
    You could say that the Book of John is all about hope.

4   The certainty and conviction in Jesus's tone are inspiring. He is being chal-
    lenged and threatened, and yet he stands confident in his calling. This fear-
    lessness does not come from his ego but from his discovery that he is close
    to the very source of life. The universe itself backs him up.

5   Psalm 82:6

6   "We have the power to change America and give a kind of new vitality to
    the religion of Jesus Christ. And we can get those young men and women
    who've lost faith in the church to see that Jesus was a serious man precisely
    because he dealt with the tang of the human mind amid the glow of the divine."
        —Martin Luther King, *The Autobiography of Martin Luther King, Jr.*, ed. Clayborne
        Carson (New York: Warner Books, 1998), 351

"No one has taken my life. I give it up on my own.[3] I have the authority to give it up and to restore it, a power I got from my Father."

Again the Jews were divided over these words, many saying, "He has a daimon and is crazy. Why do you listen to him?" Others said, "Those aren't the words of someone who's possessed. A daimon can't clear the eyes of the blind."

That year the Festival of the Dedication took place in Jerusalem. It was in the winter and Jesus walked into the temple through the portico of Solomon. The Jews circled round him and asked, "How long do we have to hold our breath? Tell us directly if you're Christos."

Jesus answered, "I told you, and you don't believe me. The things I do in my Father's name confirm me. But you don't believe me because you're not my sheep. My sheep hear my voice. I know them and they follow me. I give them eternal life. They never die. No one will take them away from me.

"My Father, who gave them to me, is greater than anyone. No one can take them from my Father's embrace.[4] The Father and I are one."

The Jews picked up stones to throw at him.

He said, "I showed you many wonders that were from the Father. Which one makes you want to stone me?"

The Jews said, "We aren't going to stone you for doing something good but for blasphemy. You're a human being pretending to be God."

Jesus said, "Isn't it written in your law, 'I said you are gods'?[5] Moses called human beings gods. And it was the word of God that came to him, a scripture that can't be contradicted. Now you're accusing someone the Father sanctified and sent into the world, calling me blasphemous because I said that I am the son of God.[6]

7   We get two related and difficult words in John: signs (*semeia*) and actions
    (*erga*). Both seem to refer to healings and miraculous deeds, but the words
    used are more ordinary. Perhaps the actions are those things Jesus does
    that indicate he is of another order altogether. They are actually deeds of
    the Father. They are not human actions but life itself showing its power to
    heal. Signs seem to point to Jesus himself. A wondrous act shows that Jesus
    embodies another and more powerful way of life. These actions are meant to
    signify this other way, the way of the kingdom.

"If what I do doesn't represent my Father's activity, then don't believe in me. But if it does, even if you don't believe in me, believe in the deeds done. Then you will understand that the Father is in me and I am in the Father."

Again they wanted to arrest him, but he eluded them. He went off beyond the Jordan to the place where John had been baptizing at first and he stayed there. Many visited him and said, "Maybe John didn't perform any signs,[7] but everything he said about this man was correct." Many people there put their trust in him.

1   This is Mary of Bethany, not Mary of Magdala. But she is a woman who
    showed her love for Jesus by rubbing him with oil.

2   Notice how close Jesus is to these three people. Some have even suggested
    that Lazarus was the beloved disciple, "the one he loved."

3   Jesus has made this point before: You must do the work of the Father while
    the opportunity presents itself. When "night" comes, it will be too late. We
    must devote ourselves to the work of saving souls from unconsciousness and
    ruined lives. In that spirit, Jesus goes off to lift Lazarus from his sleep, death,
    or unconsciousness. Lazarus serves as an image both of Jesus's death and the
    general death of the soul that is his mission to restore to life.

Chapter 11

In the town of Bethany, where Mary and her sister Martha lived, a man named Lazarus was seriously ill. This Mary is the woman who rubbed oil on the teacher and wiped his feet with her hair.[1] Lazarus was her brother.

The sisters informed Jesus, "Sir, listen, this man here, someone you love very much, is seriously ill."

When Jesus heard this he said, "The sickness isn't fatal. It's an opportunity to celebrate God and for the son of God to be more appreciated."

Jesus loved all three—Martha, Mary, and Lazarus.[2] When he learned that Lazarus was ill, he stayed where he was for two more days and then said to his followers, "Let's go back to Judea." But his followers warned him, "Rabbi, the Jews were just recently looking for a way to stone you. Are you sure you want to go back there?"

Jesus answered, "Aren't there twelve hours of daylight? If a person walks in the daylight, he doesn't trip over anything. He sees with the light of this world. But if someone walks at night, he stumbles because he has no light."[3]

Then he said, "Our friend Lazarus is asleep. I'm going so I can wake him from his sleep."

The followers said, "But, sir, if he's only asleep, he'll wake up."

Jesus was referring to his death, while they thought he was speaking literally about sleep. Jesus spoke plainly. "Lazarus is dead. For your sake, it's good that I wasn't there, so that you can trust. Let's go to him."

Thomas, known as Didymus, said to the other followers, "Let's go, too, so we can die with him."

4 Martha and Mary are often seen as different types of responses to Jesus. Here Martha takes the initiative to meet Jesus as he is arriving. That response could indicate there is no time to waste, no time to wait to understand every detail of the gospel message. Martha is going out to witness the resurrection of life that Jesus makes happen. In contrast, Mary, perhaps the more mystical and introverted of the sisters, stays behind. The Gospel reminds us that it was she who wiped Jesus's feet with her hair. She is not the activist as much as the quiet but equally devoted lover of Jesus and his message.

5 Martha understands the central message of John's Gospel, that Jesus derives his power from his closeness to the Father. She also knows that Jesus brings humanity to life. She is going out to behold resurrection, the story of Lazarus being a parable for this main teaching.

6 Jesus says plainly that he is resurrection and life. Think of these terms in relation to the deathly state of society with its wars and self-centeredness. Jesus can resurrect this body politic and offer the principle of life rather than the condition of death.

7 "For John's gospel, the process of general resurrection is incarnated in the event of Lazarus's resuscitation.... But I can imagine peasants all over Lower Galilee who would have said with equal intensity that Jesus brought life out of death and would not have been thinking of the heavenly future but the earthly present. Life out of death is how they would have understood the Kingdom of God, in which they began to take back control over their own bodies, their own hopes, and their own destinies."
    —John Dominic Crossan, *Jesus: A Revolutionary Biography* (San Francisco: HarperSanFrancisco, 1994), 95

When Jesus arrived, he discovered that Lazarus had been in the tomb for four days already. Bethany was only two miles from Jerusalem, and many Jews had come to Martha and Mary to comfort them because of their brother.

When Martha heard that Jesus was on his way, she went out to meet him while Mary stayed in the house.[4]

Martha said to Jesus, "Sir, if you had been here, my brother wouldn't have died. But even at this point, I know one thing: 'What you ask of God, he will give you.'"[5]

Jesus said, "Your brother will recover."

Martha said, "I know that he will rise again in the resurrection on the last day."

Jesus said, "I'm the resurrection and the life.[6] Whoever trusts in me will live, even if he dies. Everyone who lives and trusts in me will never die. Do you believe this?"[7]

She said, "Yes, sir. I believe that you are Christos, the son of God, who has come into our world."

After saying this, Martha went and called Mary, her sister, quietly. "The teacher is here and is asking for you."

When Mary heard this, she got up immediately and went to him. Jesus still had not arrived in the town but was far off where Martha had met him. The Jews had been with her in the house, comforting her. They noticed that Mary got up quickly and went out, so they followed her, thinking that she was going to the tomb to mourn.

8 Hear the many layers of meaning in this sentence. If Jesus is present, whose teaching can restore life and vitality, then we and our families will be fully alive.

9 Look closely at the Greek word here, *enebrimesato*, translated here as "deeply moved." The *brim* is from Brimo, a name given to Persephone and Hekate, the goddesses of the underworld. Jesus's emotions are deep in the underworld of his soul, and they have to do with the death of his friend.

10 Notice that the motive for resurrection is love. Jesus is not out to prove himself and win converts for their own sake. He brings new life. Our job, too, could be to bring life out of love where there is death.

11 Our world is really dead and reeks of decayed ideas, experiments, and ways of life. This sensual detail of the smell penetrates through the edges of the story and we sense the decomposition of society.

12 These may be words of ritual, as many commentators have pointed out. As Rudolf Steiner writes, "In Lazarus Jesus accomplished the great miracle of the transformation of life in the sense of ancient traditions. Through this event Christianity is linked with the Mysteries. Lazarus had become an initiate through Christ Jesus himself. Thereby Lazarus had become able to rise into the higher worlds. He was at the same time both the first Christian initiate and the first to be initiated by Christ Jesus himself" (Steiner). Rites of passage often include symbolic death and rising. The participant may be buried under leaves or have his eyes covered until the resurrection and new birth.

But Mary went out to Jesus and, when she saw him, fell at his feet. "Sir, if you had been here, my brother wouldn't have died."[8]

When Jesus saw her and saw the Jews who had come with her, all of them crying, he was deeply moved[9] in spirit and grieved.

"Where have you put him?" he asked.

They said, "Sir, come and see.

Jesus, too, cried then, and the Jews said, "Look how much he loved Lazarus."[10]

But a few complained. "Couldn't this man who cleared the eyes of the blind man have kept him from dying?"

Jesus still felt very sad. He went to the tomb, a cave with a stone lying against it, and said, "Take the stone away."

Martha said, "Sir, he's been dead for four days. By now there will be a strong smell."[11]

Jesus said, "Didn't I tell you that if you have trust, you will see the glory of God?"

They took the stone away and Jesus raised his eyes and said, "Father, thank you for listening to me. I know that you always listen. I say this for the benefit of these people around me, that they may believe that you sent me."

After he had spoken, he cried out loudly, "Lazarus, come out."[12]

Then the man who had died walked out of the tomb. He was bound hand and foot with cloth wrappings. Even his face was wrapped in fabric. Jesus said, "Take those wrappings off and free him."

Many of the Jews who had come with Mary saw what he had done and put their trust in him. But some went to the Pharisees and told them everything.

13 It is true. One reason some people reject the philosophy of love that Jesus teaches is that our way of life may not survive. Our institutions are not set up to support the values of the Gospels. It is nearly impossible to imagine a future where love, community, and genuine humility would be the norm.

14 Jesus's death is the culmination of a life given to teaching and embodying a unique saving message. It is a key moment in the history and story of humanity's spirituality. It could unite us all in the common effort to make a peaceful and creative world.

The chief priests and the Pharisees called for a meeting of the council. They said, "What are we going to do? This man is performing many meaningful wonders. If we let him go on like this, everyone will believe in him, and the Romans will come and take away our positions and our nation."[13]

One of them, Caiaphas, the high priest of that year, said, "You don't know anything. You don't understand that it's better for one man to die for the people so that the entire nation doesn't vanish." He wasn't just speaking as himself. He was the high priest that year and his words were prophetic: Jesus was indeed going to die for the country. And not just for the country, but to unite the children of God who were scattered everywhere.[14]

From that day on they made plans to assassinate Jesus. So Jesus no longer walked in public among the Jews. He left there and went to an area near the wilderness, to a city called Ephraim, and he stayed there with his followers.

Passover was approaching and many people were going to Jerusalem, leaving the countryside, to purify themselves for the festival. They looked around for Jesus but standing there in the temple some said, "What do you think? Will he attend the festival?"

The chief priests and the Pharisees had instructed the people that if anyone knew where Jesus was, he was to report it. They wanted to arrest him.

1 Spikenard comes from a flowering plant of the valerian family and is found
   in Nepal, China, and India. It has bell-shaped flowers, and its underground
   stems are crushed and distilled into an aromatic essential oil, amber-colored
   and thick. The oil is used as a perfume, an incense, a sedative, and an herbal
   medicine (Dalby).

2 "Although Mary of Bethany is also a disciple, she symbolizes the essentially
   contemplative aspect of the spiritual life and, as the sister of Lazarus, has a
   mystical premonition of Christ's death."
       —Susan Haskins, *Mary Magdalen: Myth and Metaphor* (New York: Riverhead
         Books, 1993), 24

3 This is a common theme in the Gospels. The religious authorities typically
   demand fasting and no demonstration of luxury or sensuality. Jesus responds
   in a moderate, Epicurean fashion: At the right time a little luxury is appropri-
   ate. Do not be so moralistic.

4 Palm branches may signify triumph, joy, or peace, and all three seem to be
   present in the procession.

Chapter 12

Six days before Passover, Jesus went to Bethany, the place where Lazarus lived, the one he had raised from the dead. They made a dinner for him. Martha was waiting on Jesus, and Lazarus was among those at the table. Mary took a pound of expensive perfume made of pure nard[1] and rubbed Jesus's feet with it and then wiped them with her hair. The house was filled with the aroma of the perfume.[2]

Judas Iscariot, one of the followers, the one who was thinking of betraying Jesus, said, "Why didn't she sell the perfume for three hundred denarii and give it to the poor?" He wasn't really concerned for the poor but was actually a thief. He kept the money box and would steal from it.

Jesus said, "Leave her alone. Let her keep it for the day of my funeral. You always have the poor among you but you don't always have me."[3]

A large group of Jews heard that he was there, and they came not only to see Jesus but Lazarus, too, the one he had raised from the dead. The chief priests had a plan to put Lazarus to death as well, since he was the reason many Jews were defecting and believing in Jesus.

The next day a big crowd showed up for the festival. When they heard that Jesus was coming into Jerusalem, they grabbed branches from palm trees and went out to greet him.[4] They sang out, "Hosanna! Blessed is he who comes in the name of the Lord, king of Israel."

5   "In classical art the ass is common in Dionysiac processions, whether car-
    rying Hephaistus, the divine smith, on his entry to Mt. Olympus, or Sile-
    nus, Dionysus' aged mentor. Both of these are drunk, and both might bear a
    remote comparison with Christ in that they are figures of wisdom, albeit of
    a very earthy kind."
        —Thomas F. Matthews, *The Clash of Gods* (Princeton, NJ: Princeton University
            Press, 1993), 45

Jesus riding on a donkey clearly fits with his entire teaching, where the last
will be first. Jesus is the antihero who avoids the glamor of the world and
enjoys the lowly gifts of an ordinary life.

6   Zechariah 9:9

7   This is another notable contact between Jesus and the Greek culture
    around him.

Jesus sat on a donkey that he had found.[5] It was written:

> *"Don't be afraid, Daughter of Sion. Look!*
> *Your king is coming,*
> *sitting on a young donkey."*[6]

At first his followers couldn't figure out what was happening. But when they saw Jesus receiving such honor, they recalled things written about him and things like this being done for him.

Some people were present who were there when he called Lazarus out of the tomb, raising him from the dead, and they didn't stop talking about him. That's why many people went out to greet him—they had heard about this wonderful sign.

The Pharisees huddled. "It's obvious that we're not very effective. The whole world has come out for him."

Some Greeks among those celebrating the festival went to Philip, who came from Bethsaida of Galilee, and asked him, "Sir, can we see Jesus?"[7]

Philip told Andrew, and Andrew and Philip told Jesus. Jesus said, "The hour for the son of man to be recognized is here. Let me tell you an important truth: Unless a grain of wheat falls into the earth and dies, it remains inactive. But if it dies, it bears fruit. Whoever loves his soul will lose it, and whoever hates his soul in this world will love it in his timeless existence.

"If someone wishes to serve me, he has to follow me. Where I am, my devotee will be there. If someone cares for me, the Father will give him honor.

"Now my soul is deeply disturbed. Should I say, 'Father, keep me from this moment'? No, this is why I have arrived at this moment. Father, all honor to your name."

At that moment a voice sounded from the sky: "I have honored it and will honor it again."

8 These pronouncements from the sky, or the heavens, are important in keeping Jesus in touch with the realm of the invisible and mysterious. As American psychologist James Hillman writes, "When the invisible forsakes the actual world—as it deserts Job, leaving him plagued with every sort of physical disaster—then the visible world no longer sustains life, because life is no longer invisibly backed. Then the world tears you apart" (Hillman).

9 Jesus's very presence, with his modeling and teaching of a new way of living, is a critique of life as it is lived in its default state; that is, according to the unconscious values of any time or place where materialism and narcissism blend in aggressive self-serving, and in nationalism, racism, and a host of other -isms.

10 Scholars give us useful information about how this talk of light and darkness may come from early presumed Gnostic sources. For a clear and brief discussion, see Raymond E. Brown, *An Introduction to the Gospel of John* (New York: Doubleday, 2003), 119. He writes, "An original man, a figure of light and goodness, was torn apart and divided into small particles of light. These particles, as human souls, were seeded in a world of darkness, and it has been the task of the demons to make them forget their heavenly origins. Then God's son is sent in corporeal form to waken these souls, liberate them from their bodies of darkness, and lead them back. He gives souls the true knowledge (gnosis) that will enable them to find their way back" (Brown).

11 Isaiah 53:1

12 Isaiah 6:10. This passage indicates that a hard heart and blindness are both illnesses in need of healing. Softening the heart and seeing more clearly are two ways to prepare for Jesus's way of life and could be two goals in a spiritual education and in spiritual therapeutics.

People who were standing nearby heard the voice and said later that it thundered. Some said that an angel had spoken.[8]

Jesus said, "This voice did not appear for me but for you. Now the world is being evaluated.[9] Now the rulers of this world will be expelled. And if I am lifted up from the earth, I will attract all people to me." He was using this kind of language to indicate the kind of death he would suffer.

The people responded, "We read in the law that Christos will stay forever. Why do you say, 'The son of man will be lifted up'? Who is this son of man?"

Jesus said, "The light is with you for just a while longer. Act while you have the light. Don't let the darkness overcome you. Anyone who walks in darkness doesn't know where he's going. While you have the light, trust in the light, become sons and daughters of light."[10]

Jesus said all of this and then went away and hid from them. Even though he displayed so many wonderful signs in plain view, they still didn't put their trust in him. This fulfilled Isaiah the prophet saying,

> *"Master, who believed what we said?*
> *Who has seen the Lord's arm?"*[11]

They couldn't put their trust in him. Again Isaiah said,

> *"He has blinded their eyes*
> *and hardened their hearts.*
> *They couldn't see with their eyes*
> *or understand with their hearts*
> *and be healed."*[12]

Isaiah said these things because he saw the Lord's majesty and testified to it.

13 This is an interesting group: those who trust the teachings of Jesus but are not public about it, perhaps afraid to be criticized by religious authorities. Today that might include people who follow the teachings without belonging to a specific religious institution or community, that is, those who are spiritual but not religious.

14 "The arrival at insight requires a basic entrance into the finite and the limited.... Christ moved down into all the realities of man to get to his Father."
   —William F. Lynch, *Christ and Apollo* (New York: Sheed and Ward, 1960), 13

15 The Greek here, *zoe aionio*, is usually translated "eternal life." *Zoe* is "life," the root of our word *zoo*. *Aion* can mean the ages, destiny, and even the era in which we live. It is also used of mythic beings that clothe us in flesh as we are becoming human. There is no easy way to translate all of this. I say "timeless" to get us away from the linear idea of eternity and to imply destiny and the psyche's reality in our lives. It is closer to the realm of dream than daily activity and more like the realm discovered in serious meditation than in practical life.

16 How do we know what the Father instructs us to say? We study the natural world to learn its laws and ways, and we learn the rules of human existence from experience and reflection. In these ways we may come to understand the ways of the universe and how to adjust to them.

In spite of this, many of the leaders put their trust in Jesus, although, because of the Pharisees, they kept quiet about it. Those who enjoyed the approval of people rather than acceptance from God might have thrown them out of the synagogue.[13]

Jesus spoke up. "Whoever believes in me ultimately doesn't believe in me but in the one who sent me. Whoever sees me sees the one who sent me. I have come as a light to the world so that anyone who puts his trust in me will not stay in darkness.[14] If someone hears my message and doesn't observe it, I won't judge him. I didn't come to judge the world but to save it. Whoever rejects me and doesn't accept my message has a judge; the words I've spoken will judge him on the last day.

"I don't speak for myself. The Father who sent me has instructed me about what to say. I understand that his instruction is about the timeless.[15] And so whatever I say, I say exactly what the Father instructed me to say.[16]

1   "The symbolic message attached to the last meal which was consumed by
     Jesus and his disciples 'before the feast of Passover' (John 13:1) is not redemp-
     tion through eating the body and drinking the blood of Jesus, the true Pass-
     over lamb, but that of humility impressed on them by the master when he
     washed the feet of his disciples (John 13:1–20)."
          —Geza Vermes, *The Changing Faces of Jesus* (New York: Penguin, 200), 22

2   This is a good way to think about our own dying, that we have come from
     God and are returning. Emily Dickinson's last letter reads, "Called back."
     Mozart's last words carry the theme forward: "The taste of death is upon my
     lips. I feel something that is not of this earth."

3   "To wash the feet, an activity paradigmatic of love, means laying down our
     own sense of unconditional value in recognition of the unconditional value
     of another. We shift the center of our lives away from ourselves as objects of
     our own attention.... We are forced to relinquish the sense of ourselves as
     isolated, atomic, selfish beings, to abandon the selves we have constituted
     by materializing past memories, thoughts, and desires into the complex arti-
     fact with which we have identified."
          —Christopher Bamford, *An Endless Trace: The Passionate Pursuit of Wisdom in the*
          West (New Palz, NY: Codhill Press, 2003), 290

4   This is a strong statement about the washing. If Peter does not submit to it,
     he will have no connection with Jesus. It seems essential. And the image of
     foot washing has several facets: being morally clean; once again using water
     for vitality; the person doing the washing is humbled in his service, a key
     theme of the teaching.

5   It seems that Jesus rarely intends anything he says to be taken literally. He
     is an everyday practical and spiritual poet. Here he lets the image of water
     and washing keep flowing. To appreciate the nuances of his ideas, you must
     grasp their poetic resonance.

Chapter 13

Before the festival of Passover, Jesus knew that his moment had come to leave this world and go to the Father. He loved his own followers in the world, loved them right to the end.[1]

During the meal, the devil placed the idea in the heart of Judas Iscariot, the son of Simon, to betray Jesus. Jesus understood that the Father had put everything in his, Jesus's, hands and knew that he had come from God and was returning.[2]

He got up from the table, put his outer clothes aside, and took a towel and tied it around him. Then he poured water into a basin and washed his followers' feet and wiped them with his towel.[3] He came to Simon Peter, who said, "Master, are you going to wash my feet?"

Jesus said, "You don't understand what I'm doing now, but you will later."

"You'll never wash my feet," Peter said.

Jesus replied, "If I don't wash your feet, you won't have any connection with me."[4]

Peter said, "Master, don't just wash my feet but my hands and head, too."

Jesus told him, "If you've taken a bath, I only need to wash your feet. You're clean. But not everyone is clean." He knew that one of them would betray him. That's why he said, "Not everyone is clean."[5]

6 "Marana, 'our Lord,' in the liturgical formula, Maranatha, 'Our Lord, come!' translated into Greek as *ho Kyrios*.... It was not merely in the name of a great teacher, not even in the name of the greatest teacher who ever lived, that Justinian built Hagia Sophia in Constantinople and Johann Sebastian Bach composed the Mass in B-Minor. There are no cathedrals in honor of Socrates."
   —Jaroslav Pelikan, *Jesus through the Centuries: His Place in the History of Culture* (New Haven: Yale University Press, 1985), 17

7 This is a clear instruction: Serve each other and keep each other morally and intellectually clean.

8 Purifying the mind, a theme much discussed in the context of this story, involves freeing our thoughts of moralism and literalism, two problems that Jesus addresses frequently. Also, we might think of the one sent not being greater than the one who sent him, as no messenger is greater than the message.

9 Psalm 41:9

10 Here we have a three-part transmission: someone I send, me, and the one who sent me. We need this direct chain so that the ones we listen to speak for Jesus accurately, and then the ultimate sender, in some way the message itself, will be accessible.

11 You must be ready for betrayal and not so innocent that you do not expect it. Even the apostles had a traitor in their number. For an excellent essay on betrayal, look at "Betrayal" in James Hillman, *Loose Ends* (Dallas: Spring Publications, 1975), 63–81.

12 The famous "beloved disciple."

When he finished washing their feet and put his clothes back on and sat at the table again, he said, "Do you know what I've just done? You call me Teacher and Lord. You're correct.[6] That's what I am. If I, your Lord and Teacher, washed your feet, you should also wash one another's feet.[7] This was an example that I gave you. You should do as I did. I tell you honestly, a servant is not greater than his master, nor is the one who is sent greater than the one who sent him. If you understand this and act on it, you'll be blessed.[8]

"I'm not talking about all of you. I know who I have selected. The scripture will be fulfilled:

"'The one eating my bread has lifted his foot against me.'[9]

"From now on I'll tell you a thing before it takes place, so when it does occur you'll believe that I am he.

"This is the truth: If you receive someone I send, you receive me. If you receive me, you receive the one who sent me."[10]

After Jesus said this, his spirit was agitated and he said, "Listen. I have to tell you, one of you is going to betray me."[11]

The followers looked at one another, uncertain about who he was referring to. One of the students, leaning on Jesus's chest, was the one he loved.[12] Simon Peter nodded to that person and said, "Who is he talking about?"

The beloved student leaned back on Jesus and said, "Master, who is it?"

Jesus said, "I'll dip a piece of food in the bowl and give it to him." So he dipped the piece of food and gave it to Judas, the son of Simon Iscariot.

After this exchange of food, Satan entered Judas, and Jesus told him, "Do what you have to do quickly."

13 "The old gods are dead or dying and people everywhere are searching, asking: What is the new mythology to be? One cannot predict the next mythology any more than one can predict tonight's dream; for a mythology is not
an ideology. It is not something projected from the brain, but something
experienced from the heart, from recognitions of identities behind or within
the appearances of nature, perceiving with love a 'thou' where there would
have been otherwise only an 'it.'"
    —Joseph Campbell, *The Inner Reaches of Outer Space: Metaphor as Myth and as
    Religion* (New York: Alfred Van Der Marck Editions, 1986), 17

14 The number three here adds intensity, mystery, and weight to the denials.

No one at the table knew why he had said this. Some thought since Judas kept the money box that Jesus was saying, "Buy what we need for the festival" or "Give something to the poor." After getting the bit of food, Judas went out right away. It was nighttime.

When Judas had gone, Jesus said, "Now the son of man has been given honor, and God will find honor in him. If God finds honor in him, God will honor him in himself and will honor him directly. Little children, I am going to be with you just a little longer. You'll look for me, but as I told the Jews, you can't come where I'm going.

"I'm giving you a new commandment.[13] Love one another, just as I have loved you. By this everyone in the world will know that you are my followers, if you love one another."

Simon Peter said, "Master, where are you going?"

Jesus answered, "You can't come where I'm going, but you'll come later."

Peter said, "Master, why can't I go along with you now? I'll give my life for you."

Jesus said, "You'll give your life for me? Let me tell you, a rooster won't crow until you have denied me three times."[14]

1 Again, Jesus is talking as though he exists on another plane. His followers have trouble understanding the level on which he is talking, not just his words. He is the spiritual poet speaking a shamanic language, implying multiple levels of existence and understanding.

2 The word usually translated as "truth" here is *aletheia*, and the best book on this subject that I know is *The Masters of Truth in Archaic Greece* by Marcel Detienne (New York: Zone Books, 1996). "Aletheia was not the opposite of 'lies' or 'falsehood.' The only meaningful opposition involved Aletheia and Lethe (forgetfulness). If the poet was truly inspired, if what he had to say was based on his gift of second sight, then his speech tended to be identified with the 'truth'" (Detienne). Therefore I translate the word for "truth" here as "deep memory," the kind of archetypal awareness that leads to a real poet's expression.

3 We tend to divide sky and earth, eternal and life, Jesus and that which fathers his vision. He is trying hard here to impress upon us that to see the eternal Tao, the father-source of everything, you can look to Jesus—to his life and his teaching.

4 The "wonders," signs (*semeia*), in John are those actions that transcend the laws and ways of the literal world. If we trust the wonders, we will find our way to the kingdom, a different way of being in this world. In the kingdom there is no egotism, narcissism, or violence. It's another way to be in this world, a kind of fourth dimension.

Chapter 14

"Don't let your heart be troubled. Trust in God and trust in me. In my Father's house there are many rooms. If there weren't, I would have told you. I am going to get a place ready for you. If I do go and prepare a room for you, I'll return and welcome you there with me. Wherever I am, you'll be there, too. You know the way I'm taking."

Thomas said, "Sir, we don't know where you're going, and so we don't know the way."[1]

Jesus said, "I am the path, the deep memory,[2] and the life. No one comes to the Father except through me. If you knew me, you would know my Father as well. From now on you will know him and will see him."

Philip said, "Sir, show us the Father and we will be satisfied."

Jesus said, "Philip, I've been with you for a long time and still you don't know me? If you've seen me, you've seen the Father. Why would you say, 'Show us the Father'? Don't you believe that I am in the Father and the Father is in me?[3] The words I'm speaking to you don't come from me but from the Father dwelling in me and doing his work. Trust me, I am in the Father and the Father is in me. You can put your faith in this because of the wonders I have done.[4]

"This is the truth: Whoever puts his trust in me and the wonders I do will also do wonders, because I'm going away to the Father. Whatever you ask for in my name, I'll get for you. The Father will find glory in the son. If you ask me for anything at all in my name, I'll do it.

5   Again, the word is *aletheia*, a deep remembering that is primarily the work
    of a poetic mind. So this "paraclete" sounds something like the daimon of
    Socrates, a holy spirit that takes you deep and guides you.

6   "In our making God knit us and 'oned' us to himself, by which 'oneing' we
    are kept as clean and noble as when we were made.... And so in our mak-
    ing, God almighty is our kindly father and God All-Wisdom is our kindly
    mother.... And in the knitting and in the 'oneing' he is our very true spouse
    and we his beloved wife."
        —Julian of Norwich, in Marcelle Thiébaux, trans., *The Writings of Medieval
        Women* (New York: Garland Publishing, 1994), 454–55

7   The Greek word for "love" here is *agape*. This is not emotional love. This pas-
    sage makes it clear that to love Jesus is to follow his teachings. It is a com-
    mon mistake to love the person and not live the teachings.

8   The gospel teaching is not really Christian; it is not the viewpoint of any
    person or sect. It is the way of nature, the law of things given to human
    beings from the origins, from the Father.

9   Obedience to the Father's will or design is a form of love. Jesus reveals the
    Father's plans exactly and shows in his own life how to live them.

"If you love me, you will be faithful to my instructions. But I'll ask the Father, and he'll give you another comforter, a paraclete, who will always be with you. He is the spirit of truth.[5] The world can't accept him because it can't see him or recognize him. You know him because he dwells inside you and will be in you. I won't leave you orphans. I'll come to you.

"After a short while the world will no longer see me, but you will. Because I have life, you will, too. On that day you'll know that I am in my Father and you are in me and I am in you.[6] Whoever has my values and observes them is the one who loves me. Whoever loves me, my Father will love, and I'll love him and reveal myself to him."

Judas (not Judas Iscariot) said, "Sir, what has happened to make you reveal yourself to us and not to the world?"

Jesus said, "If a person loves me, he'll live out my teaching. My Father will love him, and we will come and dwell with him. The person who doesn't live out my teaching doesn't love me.[7] The teaching you hear is not mine. It's from the Father who sent me.[8] I've said all this to you while I was living among you. But in my name the Father will send the comforter, the paraclete, or the holy spirit. He'll teach you everything and help you remember everything I've said to you.

"I'm leaving my peace behind with you. I'm giving you my peace. But I don't give it to you in a worldly way. Don't let your heart be troubled and don't be afraid. You've heard what I said: I go away and will come to you. If you really love me, you'll be happy that I'm going to the Father, who is greater than I.

"I've told you all this before it happens, so that when it all takes place you'll trust it. I won't say much more, because the worldly leader is coming, and he has nothing to do with me. I do exactly what the Father requires of me so that the world can see that I love the Father.[9]

"Get up now, let's get away from here."

1   Many commentators have seen this line as an explicit connection between Jesus and the god Dionysus—the Dionysian Jesus. Dionysus was a god who was dismembered, resurrected, and his essential nature seen in the vine and grape, which is crushed and resurrected as a more intense version of itself. In other words, wine is an image of the kingdom, as we saw at the Last Supper and at Cana. Jesus is Dionysian in that he offers an intensifying of life through his death and, as at Cana, his way of life is intoxicating, like wine, compared to the self-centered default standard of humanity.

2   The Greek word is *katharoi*, as in the Anglicized word "catharsis."

3   "All Things are comprehended in their Eternal Forms in the Divine body of the Saviour the True Vine of Eternity The Human Imagination."
     —William Blake, *The Complete Poetry and Prose of William Blake*, ed. David V. Erdman (Berkeley: University of California Press, 1982), 555

4   "The real mystery of Christ is a twofold one, that 'Christ is nothing, never forget it, Christianity' (Kierkegaard), he emptied himself, obliterated himself, painted himself white on white; the other is the mystery of the Holy Spirit which is the face of Christ as that face is realized in the art-work which is each one of us."
     —Mark Patrick Hederman, *Walkabout* (Blackrock, Ireland: Columba Press, 2005), 301

5   If we live the kingdom vision and values, the world itself benefits. The very root of reality's meaning increases on account of our good action.

6   In this section of John, again we see the Dionysian pattern in Jesus's teaching. Writing to Sigmund Freud, C. G. Jung made an eloquent appeal for the return of the Dionysian: "To ever so gently transform Christ back into the soothsaying god of the vine, which he was, and in this way absorb those ecstatic instinctual forces of Christianity for the one purpose of making the cult and the sacred myth what they once were—a drunken feast of joy where man regained the ethos and holiness of an animal" (Jung).

Chapter 15

"I am the real vine[1] and my Father is the vineyard caretaker. Any branch on me that doesn't bear fruit, he pulls off. Every branch that bears fruit he prunes so it will bear more fruit. You are already pruned clear[2] because of the teaching I've given you. Live on me and I will live on you. The branch can't bear fruit by itself. It has to live on the vine. You can't either, unless you live on me. I'm the vine and you're the branches.[3] Whoever lives on me and I on him bears an abundance of fruit.[4] But apart from me you can't do anything. If a person doesn't live on me, he will be tossed away like a dried-up branch. These dried-up branches will be collected and tossed in the fire.

"If you live in me, and my teaching lives in you, ask anything you want and it will be done. My Father gains honor if you bear fruit.[5] So show that you are my followers. As the Father has loved me, I have also loved you. Dwell in my love.[6]

7   Notice that the power or energy of this connection among Jesus, Father, and person is not virtue or belief but love. The word used several times here is a variant of *agape*, a love that inspires community.

8   Friendship is an achievement here, something of immense value. Here we find the culmination of Jesus's Epicureanism, his love of life, shown in his love for his friends.

9   Friends share each little step in the discovery of how things are and the way to be, that is, the Father's will or the laws of nature and of life.

10 Here we run into a fundamental contradiction: The more you discover and live by the laws of nature in your world and in yourself, the more the world will perceive you as an alien or a betrayer.

11 It is essential to remember that Jesus's teaching, every word, is the expression of an eternal, timeless, archetypal underlay of surface life. He speaks to the psyche, as a poet and spiritual visionary, as the mouthpiece of the Father, that hidden source of life, *deus absconditus*.

But the accent need not be on the hiddenness of God. Here we see a strong appeal from Jesus to listen to his teachings and discover a timeless existence, not merely a materialistic and unconscious way of life. The idea comes through in the writings of the fifteenth-century theologian Nicholas of Cusa, who first emphasized the hidden God. In his later writings, he explains, "God is the ultimate active, creative force—the power that is immanent in all being and thought. [Man] remains a *viator*, one who is infused with a special power. Acting in the image and presence of the divine creator power, he makes his own, infinitely potential and actual human world" (Watts).

"If you observe my prescriptions, you'll dwell in my love, just as I have honored my Father's commandments and dwell in his love. I say all this to you so that my happiness may be in you and that your happiness will be complete.[7]

"Here is my commandment: Love one another just as I have loved you. A person can have no greater love than to give up his life for his friends. You are my friends if you do what I require of you. I will no longer refer to you as servants, because a servant doesn't understand what his master is doing. I call you friends,[8] because I've let you know anything I've heard from my Father.[9]

"You didn't choose me. I chose you. I nominated you to go and bear fruit and have fruit that will last. Whatever you ask from the Father in my name he'll give to you. What I ask of you is that you love one another.

"If the world has no use for you, know that it rejected me before it rejected you. If you were at home in this world, the world would love you as one of its own. Since you are not this-worldly—remember, I pulled you out of the world—the world hates you.[10]

"Remember what I taught you: 'A servant is not greater than his master.' If they got me out of the way, they'll get rid of you. If they respect my ideas, they'll respect yours, too. They'll treat you this way because of my name. They don't understand who it was that sent me.[11] If I had not come and taught them, they wouldn't have gone wrong, but now they have no excuse for going wrong.

12 Psalm 69:4

13 Once again, the word is *aletheia*, with all the associations of poetics and deep memory mentioned previously.

"Whoever hates me hates my Father, too. If I hadn't done the wonderful things for them that no one else did, they wouldn't have gone wrong. But now they have seen me and hated me, and my Father as well. They've done this in fulfillment of the words written in their law:

"They hated me without a good reason.'[12]

"The helper is the spirit of deep understanding.[13] I will send him to you from the Father. He comes from the Father. He will speak on my behalf, and you will, too, because you've been with me from the beginning."

1   This inside/outsider motif is important in our contemporary world. Some
    judge others because their spiritual insights do not match established ones.
    But Jesus's students must understand that they are outsiders in this way. They
    do not have a place in the institutions because they directly obey the Father's
    laws, the ways of the natural world and of human nature.

2   Here John's Gospel speaks of a paraclete, an advocate, counselor, or com-
    forter that will be present when Jesus is no longer there physically. You can
    see this as a holy spirit or an aspect of the divine or the universe supporting
    your life. You may also understand the paraclete as a guiding spirit remain-
    ing around Jesus's teaching after he is gone.

    Jesus's vision and teaching are also permanently present as a gauge for the
    way culture unfolds. Will it live by love and in community? Or will it con-
    tinue to abide by much lower values such as self-service and conflict?

Chapter 16

"I've told you all this to keep you from faltering. At the synagogue they'll treat you like outsiders.[1] The time is coming when, if they kill you, they'll think they're doing God a good service. They'll do all this because they don't know me or the Father. I tell you this so that, when the time comes, you'll remember that I warned you. I didn't say this at first because then I was entirely with you. But now I'm on my way to the one who sent me.

"You haven't asked me, 'Where are you going?' But because of what I've said, your hearts are heavy. The truth is, it's better for you that I go away. If I don't, the comforter won't come. If I go, I'll send him to you.

"When he comes, he'll evaluate the world—its moral ignorance, moralism, and judgment: moral ignorance, because it doesn't put its trust in me; moralism, because I'm going to the Father and you'll no longer see me; judgment, because the leaders of this world have been evaluated."[2]

"I have much more to tell you, but you couldn't bear it all now. When the spirit of truth comes, he'll guide you and give you wisdom. He won't speak on his own. He'll speak only what he hears. He'll reveal to you what is to be.

"He'll honor me, as he takes from me and reveals it all to you. Everything the Father has is mine. That's why I say that the comforter will take from me and reveal it to you. In just a little while now, you won't see me. A little while longer, and you will see me."

3   The death of Jesus is a blow to anyone who places his or her hope and trust
    in him. The death is historical, but it also takes places within anyone who
    wants to live the life Jesus lays out. Christianity has not always been a good
    advocate for Jesus's teachings, and the individual person may not always
    keep the basic teaching and radical values in mind. The Jesus consciousness
    goes away. But it can always resurrect, and then we have the added comfort
    and advantage of the special spirit around Jesus and his words that can sus-
    tain us and offer guidance.

4   This is an important self-reflection within the text, a meta-reflection, you
    might say, where Jesus reveals the genre of his teaching. His students often
    have trouble distinguishing fact from metaphor, and this has been the case
    for centuries. Some people do not like talk of metaphors because they are
    afraid that the teaching will be diminished, reduced to just figures of speech.
    But if you read carefully Jesus's own statements on the subject, you see that
    he wants to be metaphorical for the subtlety and depth he intends. In this
    passage he seems to say, "All right. No more metaphors. I will try to be
    plain."

His followers said, "What's he saying? 'A little while and you won't see me, and then a while longer and you will'? And then, 'because I go to the Father'? What does he mean, 'a little while'? We don't know what he's talking about."[3]

Jesus was aware that they had questions, and so he said, "Are you wondering about what I said, 'A little while, and you won't see me, then a while longer, and you will'? I tell you the truth: You will cry and grieve while the world rejoices. You will be sad, but your sadness will turn into joy.

"When a woman is in labor, she's in pain because her time has come. But when her baby is born, she doesn't remember the pain because of her joy at the baby coming into the world. You'll grieve now, but I'll see you again and your heart will fill with joy, and no one will take that joy away from you.

"At that time, you won't ask me anything. But I assure you that if you ask the Father for anything in my name, he'll give it to you. Until now you've asked for nothing in my name. Now ask and you'll receive and your happiness will be complete.

"To describe these matters I've used metaphors and old sayings. But the time is coming when I will no longer use figures of speech. I'll tell you plainly about the Father.[4] At that time you'll call my name and ask, and I can't say that I'll petition the Father on your behalf. The Father himself loves you because you've loved me and have believed that I came from the Father. I came from the Father into the world. I'm leaving the world now and going back to the Father."

His followers said, "Yes, now you're speaking plainly and not in metaphors. Now we are convinced that you know everything and don't need anyone asking you questions. Because of this we believe that you came from God."

Jesus said, "You believe now? Well, a time is coming, and in fact has already come, for you to be separated, each one going to his own home, leaving me on my own. But I'm not really alone because the Father is with me.

5   With the Greek *nenikeka*, meaning "overcome" and translated here as "achieved
    something," we have yet another reference to the Greek gods. Notice the
    name Nike, the Greek goddess of victory, in that word. Jesus has a victory in
    relation to the "default" world that we know so well. Yet we know only too
    well that the creation of a real human community, not divided by religious
    and national boundaries, is still only a dream. The fact that Jesus's vision is
    still alive and thriving in certain areas offers some victory, but that victory
    is not complete.

    According to the deep-thinking scholar Károly Kerényi, Nike is an aspect
    of the civic goddess Athena. She is the positive, bright, and successful side
    of Athena, and for that reason I translate *nenikeka* as "achievement" rather
    than "victory." It would be a mistake to think of Nike only in terms of mili-
    tary victory. She is the feminine side of being creative and successful.

"I've told you all this so that in me you may find peace. In the world you will meet up with trouble, but have courage. I have achieved something[5] in the world."

1 Once again I translate this phrase as "eternity in life" rather than "eternal life." The latter is often taken to refer to the afterlife. My phrase suggests an awareness of timeless dimension in the life we live. It is this timeless dimension that Jesus speaks to in all his teaching and that is the realm of the Father.

2 This is a special word, *work*. Not unlike the opus of alchemy, the work of the soul and spirit is to create a meaningful life, to transform the raw material of a life into a sparkling, effective, and spiritual achievement.

3 This passage reads like a checklist of the things Jesus had to achieve in his brief ministry. His people are prepared and know what they need to know, now that he is departing. Words such as these remind us of the beginning of the Gospel: "To begin, there was the Logos. And the Logos was close to God.... The Logos took flesh."

4 This is a strong statement about human community. Jesus prays that human solidarity be patterned on the deep tie between Jesus and the Father. We have heard from him all along how mystical, profound, and effective that unity is.

Chapter 17

Jesus finished speaking, lifted his eyes to the sky, and said, "Father, the time has come. Praise your son, so the son may praise you. You gave him authority over all humanity so that everyone you entrusted to him may have eternity in life.

"Eternity in life[1] consists in knowing you, the one real God, and knowing Jesus Christos, the one who was sent. I honored you on earth by completing the work[2] that you gave me to do. Now, Father, give both me and you esteem and all the honor I had with you before the world came into existence.

"I have revealed your name to the people of the world you entrusted to me. They were yours and you gave them to me, and they have honored your mystery. At this point they know that everything you've given me does indeed come from you. I've given them the very words that you gave me. They accepted them and really understand that I came from you. They believe that you sent me.[3]

"I approach you on their behalf, not for the world but for those you have given me. They're yours, and everything that is mine is yours and yours is mine. I have found glory in them. I'm no longer in the world, but they are, and I am coming to you. Holy Father, take care of them in your name, the name you gave me, so that they will be one as we are one.[4]

"When I was with them, I cared for them in your name, the name you gave me. I protected them, and only one was lost, the son of devastation, thus fulfilling the scripture.

5   *Worldly* refers to the usual way of life: self-centered, anxious, xenophobic, neurotic, consuming, obsessive. Jesus pictures a realm entirely different, where love, friendship, and community prevail.

6   Love wiped the rust from the mirror of my heart
    and suddenly I saw the mysteries....
    Is it possible that I am the second Jesus?
        —Gharib Nawaz (1142–1236), Sufi master; adaptation mine, based on *The
        Drunken Universe: An Anthology of Persian Sufi Poetry*, trans. Peter Lamborn
        Wilson and Nasrollah Pourjavady (Grand Rapids: Phanes Press, 1987)

    Jesus insists that his teachings are not just his opinions and ideas. They represent the laws of the cosmos. To be in tune with them is to be healed and full of joy.

7   This statement helps us understand all this talk about Jesus and the Father. Their connection and the meaning of Jesus's teachings are all about the very nature of things, life in its ultimate origins, not a matter of historical developments or the limited teachings of a church or religion.

    The Tao Te Ching expresses similar ideas, as in this selection from chapter 4:

    The Tao
        Pours out everything into life—
    It is a cornucopia
        That never runs dry.
    It is the deep source of everything—
        It is nothing, and yet in everything ...
    It has been shaping things
        from before the first being,
    from before the beginning of time. (Laozi)

"Now I'm coming to you. I'm saying these things while liv-ing so that my happiness may be fulfilled in them. I gave them your teaching, and the world hated them because they aren't worldly, just as I'm not worldly. I'm not asking you to take them out of the world but to protect them from the wicked. They are not worldly, just as I'm not worldly.[5]

"Make them holy by remembering what is. Your teaching is that deep memory. Just as you sent me into the world, I have sent them. It is for them that I make myself holy, that they may be holy in the deep teaching. I don't approach you only on behalf of these people but also for those who trust in me through their teaching, that they may all be one, just as you, Father, are in me and I in you; that they, too, may be in us and so that the world will believe that you sent me.[6]

"The honor you have given me I gave to them, so that they may be one, just as we are one. I in them and you in me, that they may find completion in unity, so that the world will know that you sent me, that you love them just as you have loved me.

"Father, I also want those you have given to me to be with me where I am, so they can see the honor you've given me. You loved me before the creation of the world.[7] Compassionate Father, although the world doesn't know you, I know you, and the ones you sent me know you. I let them know your name and will continue to make it known, so that the love between you and me may be in them, and I in them."

1   The Irish writer John Moriarty sees this ravine as a significant symbol of
     Jesus going down archeologically into the history of the world and deep
     into the human psyche to redeem it. "Christ in Gethsemane is Christ Grand
     Canyon deep in the world's karma.... He is redemptively inheriting all that
     he inwardly is, all that we inwardly are. It is up through a world, up through
     a psyche, redemptively integrated he climbs, all the way up to a summit
     called Golgotha" (Moriarty).

2   Peter often represents that element in a human being that acts first and
     thinks later. He is impetuous and in this case violent. Jesus reminds him that
     sometimes you must let fate unfold.

Chapter 18

After Jesus spoke, he went with his followers across the ravine of Kidron.[1] He went into a garden there with his students. Judas, the betrayer, knew the spot, for Jesus had often met there with them all. Judas went and got a band of Roman soldiers and officers from the chief priests and Pharisees and arrived there with torches and lamps and weapons.

Jesus saw everything that was about to happen to him. He stepped forward and said, "Who are you looking for?"

They said, "Jesus the Nazarene."

He said, "I'm the one."

Judas, the betrayer, was standing there among them. When Jesus said, "I'm the one," they pulled back and fell to the ground.

Jesus asked them again, "Who are you looking for?"

They said, "Jesus the Nazarene."

Jesus said, "I told you that I'm the one. If you're looking for me, let these others go." Here he was fulfilling the words he had uttered, "I didn't lose one of those you gave me."

Simon Peter had a sword. He drew it out and struck the high priest's servant, slicing off his right ear. The servant's name was Malchus.

Jesus told Peter, "Put the sword in its sheath. Must I not drink the cup the Father has given me?"[2]

The Roman soldiers and the commander and officers of the Jews arrested Jesus and bound him and took him to Annas first. He was the father-in-law of Caiaphas, the high priest that year. Caiaphas was the person who had told the Jews that it was better for one man to die for the people.

3   The fire is an interesting detail. Peter is getting comfortable in the world
    that is not the one Jesus has been teaching him. From that comfort he denies
    that he knows Jesus. Before, in John's Gospel, Jesus had been saying repeat-
    edly that his followers knew him and knew the Father through him. Now
    Peter says he does not know Jesus.

4   The rooster crows in the morning to signal the beginning of a new day.
    Similarly, Peter's denial initiates him into a significant shadow aspect of his
    character. We all have dark places in us, and his appears to be his tendency
    to become comfortable in the unconscious world. His denial, specifically his
    awareness of his denial, wakens him not only to his weakness but also to the
    place in him where he can come alive and enter the world more consciously.
    C. G. Jung points out that the cock is also a solar animal and signals Peter's
    ascent to leadership (Jung).

Simon Peter followed Jesus, along with another of the friends. He knew the high priest and went in with Jesus to the high priest's court. Peter stood outside the door. The other man went and spoke to the doorkeeper and let Peter in. A slave girl who watched the door said to Peter, "Aren't you also one of that man's followers?"

"No," he said, "I'm not."

Slaves and officers were standing around a charcoal fire. It was cold and they were warming themselves. Peter was standing with them, getting warm.[3]

The high priest interrogated Jesus about his followers and his teaching.

Jesus responded, "I've spoken openly to the world. I always taught in synagogues and in the temple, where Jews assembled. I never spoke in secret. Why are you asking me these questions? Ask those who listened to me. They know what I said."

When he spoke this way, one of the officers standing close by struck him and said, "Is this the way to speak to the high priest?"

Jesus said, "If I have misspoken, say so. But if I spoke properly, why did you hit me?"

Annas sent him bound to Caiaphas, the high priest.

Simon Peter was still standing and warming himself. People said to him, "You're one of his followers, aren't you?"

He denied it. "I'm not."

One of the slaves of the high priest, a relative of the man whose ear Peter had cut off, said, "Didn't I see you in the garden with him?"

Peter again denied it, and a rooster crowed.[4]

5   This dialogue seems to come from Orwell's *1984*. It does not say anything, and it rejects all responsibility at the cost of a precious life. We are entering into the astounding drama of the trial and execution of Jesus, whose only crime was to present a saving recipe for the human race.

6   Who says my poems are poems?
    My poems aren't poems!
    Once you get that my poems aren't poems
    Then we can start talking about poems.
        —Zen Master Ryokan, in Nelson Foster and Jack Shoemaker, eds., *A New Zen Reader* (Hopewell, NJ: Ecco Press, 1996), 344

    Once you get the idea that the kingdom of Jesus is not a kingdom, we can start talking about kingdoms. Are you the king of the Jews? Of the Jews, yes, and all other people, too. Also, king of the individual who is trying to live successfully on this planet, advising him or her how to be cured, how to find meaning, how to know what to do.

7   For a rich background to this translation, "profound mysteries" instead of "truth," again consult Marcel Detienne, *Masters of Truth in Ancient Greece* (New York: Urzone, 1996).

8   "Our time has brought the fall of rationalism and a new turning to the mystery. The humanization of religion had progressed so far that, finally, there was no religion left. For this reason many doubted religion, which no longer held them with any inward grasp, did not bind them, was no longer something greater than they. Others, with more justification, have returned to a richer belief."
        —Odo Casel, *The Mystery of Christian Worship* (New York: Crossroad, 1999), 5

9   The people choose a thief instead of Jesus. Then Jesus goes off to be crucified between two thieves. Paul wrote in 1 Thessalonians 5:2 that "the day of the Lord will arrive, as you know only too well, like a thief in the night." Through their myth of Hermes, the Greeks understood theft in a deep way. Hermes served the soul with his habit of taking things away, such as faulty beliefs and understandings. Jesus is like Hermes in some ways. They share a common interest in language and storytelling, and perhaps also a deep kind of thieving. Jesus threatens people because he takes away standard assumptions and offers a substitute philosophy of life.

They led Jesus from Caiaphas into the Praetorium. It was early. They didn't go into the Praetorium so as not to be defiled and forbidden to eat the Passover.

Pilate came out and said, "What charge do you have against this man?"

They said, "If he weren't a criminal, we wouldn't have brought him to you."[5]

Pilate said, "Take him yourselves. Indict him by your law."

The Jews said, "We're not allowed to put a person to death."

This fulfilled Jesus's words indicating what kind of death he would suffer.

Pilate went back into the Praetorium and summoned Jesus and said, "Are you the king of the Jews?"

Jesus said, "Are you asking me this yourself, or did others say this about me?"

Pilate answered, "I'm not a Jew, am I? Your own people and the chief priests handed you over to me. What have you done?"

Jesus said, "My kingdom is not of this world. If my kingdom were worldly, then my attendants would fight and I wouldn't be handed over to the Jews. In fact, my kingdom is not in this reality."[6]

Pilate said, "But you're a king?"

Jesus said, "You're right. I am a king. For this I was born and for this I have come into the world, to speak of profound mysteries.[7] Anyone in touch with those profound mysteries hears what I say."[8]

Pilate said, "What do you mean by 'profound mysteries'?"

Having spoken, he went back to the Jews and said, "I find him not guilty. But you have a custom of releasing someone at Passover. Would you like me to release the king of the Jews to you?"

"No," they shouted. "Not him. Barabbas." Barabbas was a thief.[9]

1   The execution begins with particularly cruel theatrics, where Jesus's kingship
    is mocked in a way that causes intense pain. Drama such as this puts mean-
    ing into the torture, revealing the deep psychosis of the tormenters. King of
    the Jews and son of God are the two images that send them into the madness
    of deep violence. It would be far less intense if they had simply caused him
    pain. Patriotism and religious fervor bring a level of sadism to punishment
    that often takes it to the very edge of human imagination.

        Here, too, we have a phrase that has rung out through the centuries:
    "Behold the Man," *ecce homo*, or as I put it, "Look! The man!" Pilate keeps his
    hands clean, time after time, and here he parades the bloody, broken body
    of the man he found innocent, treated like a clown rather than the savior of
    the human race.

        David L. Miller writes about Christ as clown: "Imagining Christ as clown
    might bring some body to a sense of soul, some feeling to spiritual thought"
    (Miller). I don't mean to demean the image of Jesus in this scene at all, but
    to point to the depth of fear and loathing in the soldiers' treatment of Jesus.

2   Notice the effective dramatic movement from Praetorium to courtyard, from
    inner and intimate to public and moblike. The inner favors innocent, and
    the outer favors guilty. It would help us all to distinguish between the times
    when we are part of a mob, thinking collectively, and when we are reflecting
    for ourselves. How important it is to reflect calmly rather than just react col-
    lectively and passionately.

Chapter 19

Pilate had Jesus whipped. Soldiers twisted together a crown made of thorns and placed it on his head and draped a purple robe on him. They came close to him and taunted him, "Hail, king of the Jews." Then they punched him in the face.

Pilate came out again and said, "Look, I'm bringing him out to you so that you understand that I do not find him guilty." So Jesus came out, wearing the crown of thorns and the purple robe. Pilate said, "Look! The man!"[1]

But when the chief priests and officers saw him, they shouted, "Crucify! Crucify!"

Pilate said, "You take him and crucify him. I find him not guilty."

The Jews replied, "We have a law, and according to that law he should die, because he made himself son of God."

When Pilate heard this remark, he was really frightened. He went back into the Praetorium and said to Jesus, "Where are you from?"[2]

Jesus didn't answer.

Pilate said, "You're not going to talk to me? Don't you know that I have the power to release you or to crucify you?"

Jesus answered, "You would not have authority over me unless it had been given to you from above. That is why the one who betrayed me to you is more guilty."

Because of this conversation Pilate tried to release him, but the Jews shouted, "If you release this man, you're not a friend of Caesar. Anyone who makes himself king is Caesar's enemy."

When Pilate heard this argument, he brought Jesus out and sat in the judgment seat in a place called "The Pavement," in Hebrew, Gaggatha. It was the day of preparation for Passover, at about the sixth hour. He told the Jews, "Behold your king!"

3   "The tree of Paradise is only a prefiguration of the cross and this cross is
    the center of the world and of the drama of man's salvation. It towers from
    Golgotha to heaven, gathering the whole world together, and was set up
    in the same place where Adam was created, where he lies buried and where
    at the same hour of the same day the second Adam was to die; and at its
    foot there stream the four rivers of Paradise."
        —Hugo Rahner, *Greek Myths and Christian Mystery* (New York: Biblo and
        Tannen, 1971), 62

4   "In the Ethiopic version of the so-called *Book of Adam and Eve*, the connection
    between Adam and the Cross is made even clearer. The dying Adam com-
    mands his son Seth to bury him in the earth after the flood. 'For the place
    where my body shall be laid is the middle of the earth, and God shall come
    from thence and shall save our kindred."
        —Hugo Rahner, "The Christian Mystery and the Pagan Mysteries," in *The
        Mysteries* (Princeton, NJ: Princeton University Press, 1955), 384

5   The religious splitting of hairs that Jesus often complains about continues up
    to his execution. Jesus was careful in his use of words and spoke largely in
    metaphors. To see religious leaders using words so cautiously and in a self-
    serving way at Jesus's death adds to the indignity.

6   Psalm 22:18. Read the whole of Psalm 22 and you will see the emotional
    background of the execution scene in the Gospel as well as key images,
    such as sharing garments without tearing them apart and a great thirst. The
    notion of not ripping apart the whole garment may suggest that in spite
    of the crucifixion, and in some way because of it, Jesus's teaching remains
    intact.

They shouted, "Take him away. Take him away. Crucify him."
Pilate said, "Will I crucify your king?"
The chief priests said, "We have no king but Caesar."
So Pilate handed him over to be crucified.

They led Jesus out and he went, carrying his own cross, to the spot known as "The Place of a Skull," in Hebrew, Golgotha.³ There they crucified him along with two other men, one on each side, Jesus in the middle.⁴ Pilate had written an inscription that they put on the cross: "Jesus the Nazarene, King of the Jews."

Many Jews read the inscription, since the place where Jesus was crucified was near the city. It was written in Hebrew, Latin, and Greek. The chief priests among the Jews said to Pilate, "Don't write 'The King of the Jews,' but rather, 'He said I am King of the Jews.'"⁵

Pilate responded, "I have written what I have written."

After they crucified Jesus, the soldiers took his outer clothes and sorted them into four piles, one for each soldier. The tunic was seamless, woven as one piece. They said, "Let's not tear it but cast lots for it to see who can have it." Thus the scripture was fulfilled: "They divided my outer clothes among them, and for my tunic they cast lots."⁶

The soldiers were occupied with these things. But standing by the cross of Jesus were his mother, his mother's sister, Mary the wife of Clopas, and Mary of Magdala. When Jesus noticed his mother and the student he loved standing close by, he said to his mother, "Dear woman, this is your son." Then he said to the student, "This is your mother." From that moment the student took her into his household.

7 "John is portraying Jesus as 'thirsting' for the chalice that his Father has asked him to drink. Thus the wine that is given him to drink is not at all a kind of insult on the part of the soldiers."
　　—Mark Patrick Hederman, *Manikon Eros: Mad, Crazy Love* (Dublin, Ireland: Veritas, 2000), 51

8 "I wish I had been with Magdalen then and with the others who were Christ's lovers, so that I might have seen with my own eyes the Passion which our Lord suffered for me."
　　—Julian of Norwich, *Showings* (New York: Paulist Press, 1978), 177

9 Remember that all these details are images as well as facts. American psychologist James Hillman writes about the young idealist, the *puer* or spirit of youth, in us all. About Jesus he says, "The bleeding of Jesus tells of love, of compassion, of suffering, and of the endless flow of the divine essence into the human world, and of the bond through blood kinship and blood mystery of the human world with the divine" (Hillman). He goes on to describe the wound as a source of healing: "'Wounder healer' refers to mutilations and afflictions that release the sparks of consciousness, resulting in an organ- or body-consciousness. Healing comes then not because one is whole, integrated, and all together, but from a consciousness breaking through dismemberment" (Hillman).

10 Psalm 34:20

11 Zechariah 12:10

Later, knowing that the ordeal was just about finished, but to fulfill the scripture, Jesus said, "I'm thirsty."[7] There was a jar of sour wine nearby. Someone put a sponge soaked in it on a hyssop branch and raised it to his mouth. After Jesus had the sour wine he said, "It's over." He bowed his head and gave up his spirit.[8]

Since it was the Day of Preparation, not wanting the bodies to stay on their crosses on the Sabbath, the Jews asked Pilate that their legs be broken and that they be carried off. So soldiers arrived and broke the legs of the first man and then those of the other who was crucified with Jesus. Coming to Jesus, they saw that he was dead and didn't break his legs. But one of the soldiers punctured his side with a spear, and instantly water and blood gushed out.[9]

This is the account of a witness, and his descriptions are accurate. He knows that he is telling the truth so that you may also believe.

All this happened to fulfill the scripture, "Not a bone of him will be broken."[10] Again, "They will look at him, whom they pierced."[11]

Later, Joseph of Arimathea, one of Jesus's followers, who consulted him in secret for fear of the Jews, asked Pilate if he could take the body of Jesus. Pilate gave his permission. He went and took away the body.

Nicodemus, who had come to Jesus by night at first, also came, bringing a mixture of myrrh and aloes weighing almost one hundred pounds. They took Jesus's body and bound it with the spices in linen cloths, according to the burial customs of the Jews.

12 The details of burial here are important. They show the ongoing care for Jesus on the part of his devotees. The ointment hearkens back to the women, such as Mary of Bethany, who rubbed his feel with oil. He is a Man of Oil, Messiah, the anointed one. Oil is one of those simple substances that serves as a powerful image for raising awareness and understanding to a new level. This is the whole point of Jesus's teaching.

In the place where he was crucified there was a garden and in it a new tomb in which no one had ever been interred. Because of the Jewish Day of Preparation and since the tomb was nearby, they placed Jesus there.[12]

1   As many have noted, this key scene gives prominence to Mary of Magdala, the first to discover signs of resurrection. It is the moment when we realize that something mysterious surrounds Jesus's death, just as it did in his origins. Logos became flesh, and now flesh becomes Logos. Jesus's absence and the absence of the dead body mark the first important discovery. He is not here as he was. Can we now expect a different kind of presence, resurrection into something like Logos?

2   Notice the three significant figures at this all-important moment in the story of Jesus: Peter, the one Jesus loved in a special way, and Mary of Magdala. Peter enters the tomb first, his prerogative, no doubt, and we learn of the curious detail of the folded linens. This was no impetuous or careless event. The resurrection is meaningful, not just a triumphant trick meant to prove something.

3   Now Mary is the third to enter the tomb. She entered that holy space of ultimate transformation and significance, was able to see what it all implied, and then she was able to shift her imagination to a point of trust and belief. This scene is an extraordinary model for any person wanting to make the fundamental shift in worldview, metanoia, that Jesus taught.

4   Mary is now at another stage in her understanding of what has happened. The meaning of resurrection does not come easily. Now we see her missing the bodily presence of her teacher and, perhaps, companion.

Chapter 20

Early morning on day one of the week. It was still dark. Mary of Magdala went to the tomb and observed that the stone had been removed from the opening. She rushed off to Simon Peter and the other student, the one Jesus loved, and said, "They've taken the master from the tomb. I have no idea where they've taken him."[1]

Peter and the other one went off to the tomb. Both were hurrying, but the other outran Peter and reached the tomb first. He stooped down and looked in at the folds of linen lying there but didn't go in.

Simon Peter arrived afterward and went into the tomb. He saw the strips of linen and the burial cloth that had been wrapped around Jesus's head. It was not lying with the linen ribbons but was folded in a place off to the side.[2]

The other one, who had arrived at the tomb first, then entered and saw and believed.[3] Up to this point they didn't understand the scripture, that Jesus had to rise from the dead. The students went home, while Mary stood outside the tomb, crying. As her tears were flowing, she bent over and looked into the tomb. There she saw two angels in white, sitting, one at the head and one at the feet, where Jesus's body had been lying.

They said to her, "Dear woman, why are you crying?"

She said, "They've taken my master away and I don't know where they've taken him."[4]

5 "Life is Phoenix-like, always being born again out of its own death. The true nature of life is resurrection; all life is life after death, a second life, reincarnation.... The universal pattern of recurrence bears witness to the resurrection of the dead."
  —Norman O. Brown, *Love's Body* (New York: Vintage Books, 1966), 206

6 This is an odd moment in the story of Jesus. He has been killed and yet has not attained the full presence he would have later. You cannot get hold of him in this condition. You must wait until you appreciate what it means to have the Logos in your world.

7 "The association [of the *Gospel of Mary* with the *Gospel of John*] would at once affirm the tradition that the Lord appeared to Mary of Magdala after his resurrection and imparted special revelation to her that allowed her to instruct the other apostles; and it would also work to 'correct' any imputation in the *Gospel of John* that Mary was less than entirely worthy of her commission as 'apostle to the apostles.'"
  —Karen L. King, *The Gospel of Mary of Magdala* (Santa Rosa, CA: Polebridge Press, 2003), 133

8 R. B. Onians (1899–1986) was a classicist at the University of London. His great life work, *The Origins of European Thought about the Body, the Mind, the Soul, the World, Time, and Fate*, contains a trove of facts on these subjects, especially in the life of the ancient Romans. He describes how a Roman might kiss a dying person to receive his soul and the stuff of his mind. Onians also cites Society Islanders and the custom for a child to "inhale the parting soul at the moment of quitting the body." These people believed that their sages owed their learning to this practice (Onians).

9 There are always those who need physical proof and others who are more open to new experiences.

After she said this, she turned and saw Jesus standing there, but she didn't know it was him.

Jesus said, "Dear woman, why are you crying? Who are you looking for?"

She assumed that he must be the gardener and said, "Sir, if you've carried him off, tell me where you've put him and I'll take him."

Jesus said to her, "Mary."

She turned and in Hebrew said, *"Rabboni,"* or "Teacher."[5]

Jesus said, "Don't embrace me. I haven't been up to the Father yet.[6] Go to my brothers and tell them, 'I am going up to my Father and your Father, my God and your God.'"

Mary of Magdala went and told the other students, "I've seen the master." She told them what he had said to her.[7]

It was evening. The first day of the week. The doors were shut where the followers had gathered—for fear of the Jews. Jesus came and stood among them and said, "Peace be with you."

Then he showed them his hands and side. They were ecstatic to see the master.

Jesus repeated, "Peace. As the Father sent me, I send you."

Then he breathed on them and said, "Accept the holy spirit.[8] If you forgive anyone's grievous mistakes, they will be forgiven. If you don't remit a person's faults, they will remain as they were."

Thomas, one of the Twelve, known as Didymus, wasn't with them when Jesus came. So the others told him, "We've seen the master." But he said, "Unless I see his hands and the marks of the nails and stick my finger into the nail holes and into his side, I won't believe it."[9]

10 The Gospels in general offer a challenge to the modern person, who is surrounded by the demand for proof and evidence and numbers. Jesus wants us to imagine an ideal world, a utopia, that is very different from the default one that is both wondrous and ugly. The Book of John asks even more: a constant awareness of a fathering guidance or rule of life, manifested in the teaching and example of Jesus. The language is mystical and idealistic. Truly, the person who can follow and trust this message is blessed.

Eight days later. The students were once again indoors and Thomas was with them. Jesus entered, even though the doors had been closed, and stood among them and said, "Peace." Then he said to Thomas, "Put your finger here. Look at my hands. Put your hand in my side. Don't be incredulous. Believe."

Thomas said, "My master and my God."

Jesus said, "You have seen me and have believed. Blessed are those who don't see and yet believe."[10]

Jesus did many other wonderful things in the presence of the students, things that are not in this book. These were written so that you might believe that Jesus is Christos, the son of God, and that, with your trust, you may be revitalized by his name.

1 "The complex Fishing for Humans is a companion piece to Walking on Water and carries exactly the same meaning and message. To row all night without Jesus is to get nowhere; to fish all night without Jesus is to catch nothing."
>   —John Dominic Crossan, *The Historical Jesus* (New York: HarperSanFrancisco, 1992), 410

2 "By means of the story of the miraculous haul of fish, the Johannine community is instructed that, under the guidance of Jesus, the community is to gather all and sundry."
>   —Raymond E. Brown, *An Introduction to the Gospel of John*, ed. Francis J. Maloney (New York: Doubleday, 2003), 315

3 "The student Jesus loved" is known as "the beloved disciple." My translation is exact, and the word for love is *agape*. This is an intriguing figure about whom many have speculated. Is it John the Apostle, an unknown follower, Lazarus, or even Mary of Magdala? I would like to nominate Mary, but the references are always masculine. The main thing is that there is someone close by who all recognize as Jesus's special friend. It is good to keep in mind this kind of love as part of the Jesus phenomenon, and not just a general love for humankind.

Chapter 21

Later Jesus appeared to his followers again at the Sea of Tiberias. It happened this way.

Simon Peter and Thomas, known as Didymus, and Nathanael of Cana in Galilee, and the sons of Zebedee and two other of the students were all together. Simon Peter said, "I'm going fishing."

They said, "We'll come with you." They went and got into a boat and that night caught nothing.[1] But at daybreak Jesus was standing on the beach, although the students didn't know who it was.

Jesus said, "Young people, you haven't caught anything, have you?"

"No," they said.

"Lower the net on the right side of the boat and you will get something."

So they lowered the net and then couldn't haul it in, it was so full of fish.[2]

The student Jesus loved[3] said to Peter, "It's the master."

When Simon Peter heard that it was the master, he put his cloak on, since he was almost naked for his work, and jumped into the water.

The others came in a little boat. They weren't far from land, about a hundred yards away, dragging a net bursting with fish.

When they got to the shore, they saw a charcoal fire set up with fish on it, and bread.

Jesus said, "Bring some of the fish you caught."

4 Why this number? Perhaps for a sense of totality. The numbers from one to seventeen add up to 153. For a clear and remarkable discussion of the geometry or gematria of the fish in the Gospels, see David Fideler, *Jesus Christ, Sun of God* (Wheaton, IL: Quest Books, 1993). This is a post-resurrection event, when one might expect a deepening of the poetic meaning in the world, when number is not a mere quantity but has qualitative meaning.

5 The word for "love" in this passage is not *agape*, as so often in the Gospels. It is a form of the word *philia*, a more intimate and personal kind of love, often used of friendship. But Jesus connects this intense, personal love with taking care of others. If you have a personal feeling of connection to Jesus, the next step is to open it to others through compassion and service.

6 The principle here is clear: If you love Jesus and his way, his Tao, you will nourish those in his charge, that is, all beings. Nourishing others, providing food for the soul, is one of the key metaphors in John's Gospel.

7 Jesus advises that you continue to love him, no matter what, and do not worry about what anyone else is doing. We each have our own place in this utopia.

Simon Peter went and pulled the net onto the shore. It was teeming with large fish, 153 of them.[4] And although there were so many, the net was not torn.

Jesus said, "Come and have breakfast." None of the group dared to ask him, "Who are you?" They knew it was the master.

Jesus took the bread and gave it to them, and the fish, too.

This was the third time that Jesus appeared to his followers after he was raised from the dead.

When they had eaten breakfast, Jesus said to Simon Peter, "Simon, son of John, do you love me more than these others?"

He said, "Yes, Master. You know that I love you."

He said, "Take care of my lambs."

A second time he said, "Simon, son of John, do you love me?"

He said, "Yes, Master. You know that I love you."

He said, "Be a shepherd for my sheep."

A third time he said, "Simon, son of John, do you love me?"[5]

Peter was frustrated to be asked for the third time, "Do you love me?" He said, "Master, you know everything. You know that I love you."

Jesus said, "Take care of my sheep.[6] Let me tell you something. When you're young you dress yourself and go wherever you want. But when you get old, you stretch out your hands and someone else dresses you. Then they take you where you don't want to go."

He said this to indicate what kind of death would honor God. After saying this, he said, "Follow me."

Peter turned around and saw the student Jesus loved behind them. This was the same one who had leaned back on Jesus's chest at supper and said, "Master, who will betray you?"

Seeing him, Peter said to Jesus, "Master, what about this man?"

Jesus said, "If I want him to stay until I come, is that important to you? Just stay with me."[7]

Word went out among the people that this follower wouldn't die. Yet Jesus didn't really tell him that he wouldn't die, but only, "If I want him to stay until I come, is that important to you?"

This is the follower who is a witness to these events. We know that his story is accurate. Jesus did many other things, which, if they were written down in all their particulars, even the whole earth, I think, couldn't hold the books that would have to be written.

Acknowledgments

My heartfelt thanks to Jean Lall, Alice O. Howell, Christopher Bamford, Pat Toomay, Hari Kirin Khalsa, George Nickelsburg, John Dominic Crossan, Rev. Marcus McKinney, Emily Wichland, Jon O'Neal, Ajeet Khalsa, John Van Ness, Deborah Jessop, and Ruth Rusca.

Notes

Introduction to Gospel

1. Translations and writings on the Gospels often include chapter and verse when passages are cited. I do not include the verse because I want the reader to have a fresh, clear experience of the text. I hope that the absence of verse numbers will intensify the feeling of reading poetry, rather than prose, for study. This means that it may be slightly more difficult to navigate the text, but I think the emphasis on the poetic is more important.

2. John G. Neihardt, *Black Elk Speaks* (New York: Pocket Books, 1959), 25.

Introduction to the Book of John

1. R. Alan Culpepper, *Anatomy of the Fourth Gospel: A Study in Literary Design* (Philadelphia: Fortress Press, 1987), 97.

2. George W. E. Nickelsburg, personal communication.

Chapter 1

2. Thomas E. Sanders and Walter W. Peek, *Literature of the American Indian* (Beverly Hills: Glencoe Press, 1973), 108.

4. Gabriel Vahanian, *Wait Without Idols* (New York: George Braziller, 1964), 230.

7. Marcel Detienne, *Masters of Truth in Archaic Greece* (New York: Urzone, 1996), 41.

Chapter 2

2. Marcus J. Borg, *The Heart of Christianity: Rediscovering a Life of Faith* (San Francisco: HarperOne, 2015), 85.

3. Origen, "Commentary on John," *Ante-Nicene Fathers: The Gospel of Peter, Apocalypses and Romances, Commentaries of Origen*, ed. Allan Menzies, vol. 9 (Peabody, MA: Hendrickson, 1994), 394.

Chapter 5

8. Shunryu Suzuki, *Zen Mind, Beginner's Mind* (New York: Weatherhill, 1973), 132.

Chapter 6

2. John Dominic Crossan, *The Historical Jesus* (New York: HarperSanFrancisco, 1992), 398.

4. Crossan, *The Historical Jesus*, 405.

10. Nikos Kazantzakis, *The Last Temptation of Christ* (New York: Bantam Books, 1961), 1.

15. Mircea Eliade, *Myth and Reality* (New York: Harper & Row, 1963), 19.

18. C. G. Jung, *Symbols of Transformation*, vol. 5, *The Collected Works of C. G. Jung*, trans. R.F.C. Hull (Princeton, NJ: Princeton University Press, 1967), 30–31.

18. James Hillman, "Betrayal," in *Loose Ends* (Dallas: Spring Publications, 1975), 69–70.

Chapter 8

8. Ralph Waldo Emerson, *Emerson in His Journals*, ed. Joel Porte (Cambridge, MA: Harvard University Press, 1982), 459–60.

Chapter 9

4. Mircea Eliade, ed., *Encyclopedia of Religion*, vol. 14 (New York: Macmillan, 1987), 37.

Chapter 11

12. Rudolf Steiner, *Christianity as a Mystical Fact* (North Charleston, SC: CreateSpace Independent Publishing Platform, 2008), chapter 7.

Chapter 12

1. Andrew Dalby, *Dangerous Tastes* (Berkeley: University of California Press, 2002), 83.

8. James Hillman, *The Soul's Code* (New York: Random House, 1996), 111.

10. Raymond E. Brown, *An Introduction to the Gospel of John* (New York: Doubleday, 2003), 119.

Chapter 14

2. Marcel Detienne, *The Masters of Truth in Archaic Greece* (New York: Zone Books, 1996), 52.

Chapter 15

6. C. G. Jung and Sigmund Freud, *The Freud/Jung Letters*, ed. William McGuire, trans. Ralph Manheim and R.F.C. Hull (Princeton, NJ: Princeton University Press, 1974), 178.

11. Pauline Moffitt Watts, *Nicolaus Cusanus: A Fifteenth-Century Vision of Man* (Leiden: E. J. Brill, 1982), 223.

Chapter 17

7. Laozi, *The Illustrated Tao Te Ching*, trans. Man-Ho Kwok, Martin Palmer, and Jay Ramsay (New York: Barnes & Noble Books, 1993), 32.

Chapter 18

1. John Moriarty, *Nostos: An Autobiography* (Dublin, Ireland: Lilliput Press, 2001), 596.

4. C. G. Jung, *Symbols of Transformation*, vol. 5, *The Collected Works of C. G. Jung*, trans. R.F.C. Hull (Princeton, NJ: Princeton University Press, 1967), 197.

Chapter 19

1. David L. Miller, *Christs* (New York: Seabury Press, 1981), 57.

9. James Hillman, "Puer Wounds and Ulysses' Scar," in *Loose Ends* (Dallas: Spring Publications, 1979), 110.

9. Hillman, "Puer Wounds and Ulysses' Scar," 117.

Chapter 20

8. R. B. Onians, *The Origins of European Thought about the Body, the Mind, the Soul, the World, Time, and Fate* (Cambridge, UK: Cambridge University Press, 1951), 172.

Suggestions for Further Reading

Brown, Raymond E. *An Introduction to the Gospel of John*. New York: Doubleday, 2003.

Culpepper, R. Alan. *Anatomy of the Fourth Gospel*. Philadelphia: Fortress Press, 1983.

Detienne, Marcel. *The Masters of Truth in Archaic Greece*. New York: Zone Books, 1996.

David L. Miller. *Christs*. New York: The Seabury Press, 1981.

Rahner, Hugo. *Greek Myths and Christian Mystery*. New York: Biblo and Tannen, 1963.

About the Author

Thomas Moore is the author of the best-selling book *Care of the Soul* and many other books on deepening spirituality and cultivating soul in every aspect of life. He has been a monk, a musician, a university professor, and a depth psychotherapist, and today he lectures widely on holistic medicine, spirituality, psychotherapy, and the arts. He lectures frequently in Ireland and has a special love of Irish culture. His most recent book is *Ageless Soul*.

He has a PhD in religion from Syracuse University and has won several awards for his work, including an honorary doctorate from Lesley University and the Humanitarian Award from Einstein Medical School of Yeshiva University. Three of his books have won the prestigious Books for a Better Life awards. He writes fiction and music and often works with his wife, Hari Kirin, who is an artist and yoga instructor. He writes regular columns for the *Huffington Post*. For more about him, visit thomasmooresoul.com.

Thomas Moore is available to speak to your group or at your event. For more information, please contact us at publicity@skylightpaths.com or at (615) 255-2665.